ANOTHER CHOICE:

A Compassionate Guide to Placing a Child for Adoption

By
Jennifer Bliss, PsyD, LCSW, LPCC
and
Ann Wrixon, MSW, MBA

DEDICATION

Jennifer dedicates this book to her amazing team at the Independent Adoption Center office in Los Angeles. She is consistently impressed and inspired by their unwavering commitment to the agency's mission and the compassion they show every day in their work with adoptive families and birthparents. She would also like to thank her husband Phil and the rest of her family for their love and support throughout the years.

Ann dedicates this book to her loving family, her husband Thom and their daughter Elizabeth. In addition, she wants to thank the entire Independent Adoption Center staff that work every day to help birth and adoptive families create lifelong connections that are in the best interests of their children.

ACKNOWLEDGEMENTS

Our first obligation and honor is to thank Leslie Foge and Gail Mosconi, the authors of the first two editions of this book, which was titled "The Third Choice: A Woman's Guide to Placing a Child for Adoption." This revised and expanded third edition would not exist without their pioneering efforts.

In addition, we would like to thank all of our colleagues who helped to proofread this book. Not only did they correct our imaginative grammar, but they also provided their insights and suggestions on every aspect of this book. Thank you to each of the following people:

- Guylaine Hubbard-Brosmer, Ph.D., M.S.W.
- Elizabeth Kwiatkowski-Wrixon
- Laura Smith
- Karen Tirlia, M.S.W.
- Mallory Winter, L.M.S.W.

Finally, we want to thank Aki Parker, M.F.A., for the beautifully designed cover art for the book.

PREFACE: A NOTE FROM THE AUTHORS

We have worked for the Independent Adoption Center (IAC) for almost a decade. Ann is the executive director and Jennifer is the national associate counseling director and the Los Angeles branch director. We are social workers with master's degrees in social work (M.S.W.). Jennifer also has a doctorate in clinical psychology (Psy.D.).

During our tenure the IAC has overseen more than one thousand adoptions. As managers at the agency, we oversee the counselors working on these placements. In addition, we have provided primary counseling services to birth and adoptive families as open adoption counselors.

Our work at IAC has influenced our values regarding adoption. We are committed to open adoption, which we define as ongoing, in-person contact between the birth and adoptive families and the adoptee. Our commitment is not just the result of our clinical observations as adoption counselors, but also our study of the large body of research documenting how birthparents, adoptees, and even adoptive parents achieve the best outcomes through open adoption.

In addition, we believe in the non-discrimination policy that the agency implemented at its inception. IAC does not discriminate against adoptive parents on the basis of sexual orientation, gender identity or expression, religion, marital status, age, race, ethnicity, national origin or any other reason that does not affect a person's ability to parent. This policy allows birthparents to have a much wider choice of possible adoptive parents for their child.

Although our values were influenced by the research on open adoption, our clinical experience, and the non-discrimination policies of the agency, the single biggest influence on our values and those of the agency is IAC Associate Executive Director, Kathleen Silber. She is an open adoption pioneer whose work over the last forty years has fundamentally changed adoption in the United States. Long before most professionals considered open adoption the best practice, Kathleen intuitively knew that open communication and a lack of secrecy built healthy families. She shared this information by co-authoring two groundbreaking books, *"Dear Birthmother"* and *"Children of Open Adoption."*

As a result of Kathleen's courageous work in breaking down the barriers that kept birth and adoptive families separate and secret from each other, today fifty-five percent of adoptions in the United States are fully open and another forty percent have at least some level of openness. All of these children grow up knowing that their birthparents made an adoption plan out of love, and that their birth and adoptive families love them deeply. This is what we want for all our children, what open adoption provides, and what Kathleen Silber has made possible.

FORWARD: LANGUAGE IN ADOPTION

Language is a powerful way to communicate ideas and values. As a culture, we acknowledge that some words are offensive to all or incite hatred and are therefore anathema. But sometimes we fail to realize that some words in certain contexts, although not universally offensive, may nonetheless convey negative messages.

This is particularly true in adoption. For example, when the term "giving up" is used, it most often refers to shedding a negative or undesirable behavior such as smoking or drinking. Accordingly, using the phrase "giving up for adoption" can implicitly send the message that something is undesirable about the child.

"Giving up" can also imply a lack of caring and planning. But in reality, birthparents go through a deliberate and demanding process to "place" their child for adoption. The process is emotionally and logistically difficult, exactly the opposite of what "giving up a child" implies. It requires great emotional maturity, resiliency, planning and foresight. It is a deeply caring choice requiring a long-term commitment.

To honor the process that birth and adoptive families undertake we want to encourage people to use positive adoption language. Below is a chart listing current common word usage with more positive alternatives:

Common Usage	Positive Adoption Language
Give up or Put up a child for adoption	Place a child for adoption
Real parents	Birthparents
Natural parents	Birthparents
Adopted child	My child
Real child	Birth child
Keeping the baby or child	Parenting

Some people consider it coercive to use the word "birthmother" before a woman makes an adoptive placement. A woman is free to change her mind until after the birth, when she signs paperwork allowing an agency or attorney to terminate her parental rights. Therefore, we use the term "expectant mother" to describe a pregnant woman who is considering adoption and "prospective birthmother" after she is matched with a prospective adoptive family. The term "prospective birthmother" allows a woman to emotionally try on the role of birthmother without making a binding commitment to placement. This can serve as "trial period" to determine if she can or wants to make a permanent plan to become a birthmother.

A Note on Quotes from Birth and Adoptive Families

Throughout the book, we use quotes from birth and adoptive families. All of the quotes are real, but the names, ages, and some identifying details of those quoted have been altered to protect the identities of these families.

CONTENTS

INTRODUCTION: AN ADOPTION RENAISSANCE

The Legacy of Closed Adoption

Before the 1970s, the practice of adoption consisted primarily of what we now call "closed" adoption. Adoption practitioners did not allow a woman who was considering placing her child to make decisions about who would adopt her child. She certainly was not allowed to meet the adopting family or learn information about them that could help her to one day find and contact the adoptive family. It was also standard practice that the birthmother and her family were not allowed to see, touch, hold, or say goodbye to the baby before placement. Often no one even told the birthmother the sex of her child.

In agency adoptions, it was common practice for a baby to go directly from the hospital to a temporary placement in a foster home while the legal issues were resolved, the health of the child was established, and social workers found a suitable potential adoptive family. Upon reaching adulthood, many adoptees found out that they had spent weeks or months in foster care before social workers placed them with their adoptive families. Current research on child development shows that children who are placed with one family from birth have the best outcomes. Moving a child, even a newborn, from foster care to an adoptive placement is not ideal.

Child welfare advocates of the late nineteenth and early twentieth centuries developed the practice of closed adoption for a variety of reasons, all rooted in the beliefs and morals of the time. During those times, society had little tolerance for single parents, unless it was the result of the death of a spouse. Closed adoption evolved from a need for privacy that would protect the reputation

1

of the expectant mother and save her and her family from the shame of an out-of-wedlock birth.

Social workers and those controlling the adoption process also believed that they, as professionals, were better equipped than the expectant mother to make decisions about what was best for the child. They did not believe that a woman, who had already made one "bad decision" by having sex outside of marriage, had the capacity or the right to decide what would be best for her child.

The professionals also believed that if an expectant mother became too involved with the adoption or with the baby—knowing who the potential adoptive family was, seeing the baby, or spending time with the child before placement—she would not be able to separate from the baby and the adoption would be too hard on her. Professionals counseled the birthmother to put this chapter of her life behind her and go on as if nothing had happened.

Another prevailing belief that supported the practice of closed adoption was the idea that babies were "blank slates" upon which the adoptive family could instill its own history, lifestyle, values, and character. This belief helped the potential adoptive family feel a sense of entitlement to the adopted child and calmed any fear that the child had inherited the birthmother's "bad" character. Unfortunately, it also did a tremendous disservice to the child by sending the implicit message that the racial, ethnic, genetic, and medical characteristics inherited from his or her birth family should be dismissed.

An Open Adoption Renaissance

In the 1970s, the practice of adoption began to undergo a profound transformation due to societal changes. A variety of factors reduced the number of expectant women forced to consider adoption, including the availability of birth control and abortion and the reduction of the social stigma previously associated with single parenting. All of these factors meant there were fewer infants available for adoption than in the past.

Around this same time, numerous adoptees placed through the traditional, closed adoption process began searching for information about their birth families and making contact with them. These adult adoptees were reporting that, while their adoptive families had raised them with love, they continued to wonder about their birth families, their background, and the reason their birthparents placed them for adoption. These adoptees felt "incomplete," with an empty place within themselves caused by not knowing the basic information non-adoptees take for granted, such as where they came from, what their family health history was, and how they came to be in their present family.

Birthparents and adoptees were beginning to speak more publicly about the painful impact that adoption had on their lives. As these voices began to emerge, a common solution began to take shape within the adoption community. Instead of abolishing adoption or classifying it as an undesirable choice born of desperation, secrecy, and shame, the process could be made more open and humane.

In this new type of adoption, the people involved could truly control the process. An expectant mother could choose the family who would parent her child. She could actually meet the new parents. A birthmother could see, hold, and spend time with her baby after the birth before placing the baby with the new parents. The birthparents, the adoptive family, and the child could stay in contact with each other following placement.

In the early 1980s, these options became available through pioneering agencies like the Independent Adoption Center and some private adoption attorneys. It quickly became clear that not only was adoption itself evolving before our very eyes, but these new elements of openness had powerful and positive effects on the future mental and emotional health of adoptees as well as the adoptive and birth families.

"I could never imagine having a complete stranger raise my baby."
                    Debbie, 17-year-old birthmother

"I couldn't stand not ever being able to see or hold my baby."
                    Julie, 24-year-old birthmother

"The thought of my child going into foster care was just too much."
                    Mona, 32-year-old birthmother

Initially some adoption professionals had a negative reaction to the change from a closed system to a more open one. These professionals expressed concern that openness in adoption might prolong the grieving and letting-go process for birthmothers, keeping them trapped in a state of quasi-parenthood, unable to move on emotionally with their lives.

Other critics believed adoptees would be confused about who their "real" parents were and would never feel grounded in their adoptive families. Some also feared the adoptive family would never feel truly entitled to parent or fully bond with the child if the birthparents or birth relatives remained in contact. Fortunately, over the last twenty years there has been substantial longitudinal research showing that these fears were unfounded (We explain the research in more detail in Chapter 15).

Open adoption is not an entirely new concept in this country. Before institutional adoptions emerged in the late 1800s, birth families would place children from unplanned pregnancies with relatives or community members. A young daughter who got pregnant without the benefit of marriage was hidden away and the pregnancy disguised under baggy clothing.

Sometimes she was sent off to visit a relative, returning alone some months later having left the baby to be raised by another family member. Sometimes an older married sister or even

4

the girl's own mother would raise the child as her own. All the family members knew the truth, but no one talked about it, and people went on with their lives in their new roles. This was not a healthy way to deal with adoption. The family secret rested most heavily on the shoulders of the adoptee, who was usually the last to know it, if she or he was ever told.

We do know from this history, however, that a birthmother is capable of relinquishing her role as mother while remaining in physical contact with the child. The lack of communication about the adoption was the source of the problems with these adoptions, not that the birthmother had contact with her birth child.

The vast majority of birthmothers we have worked with as adoption counselors say that by participating actively in their adoption plan—choosing and meeting the new parents; seeing, holding, and spending time with the baby before placement; and establishing ongoing contact with the adopting family—they are able to take greater ownership of their choice.

They feel more confident, grieve their loss more concretely, feel more complete about their decision, and have a sense of pride, accomplishment, and peace of mind knowing they did their best to create the life they envisioned for their child. Current research on psychosocial outcomes for women who place children in open adoptions confirms our clinical observations that open adoption is the healthiest option for birthmothers (see Chapter 15 for information on this research).

CHAPTER 1: CHOOSING ADOPTION

A Personal Choice

Men and women, whether single or married, financially stable or struggling, childless or parenting, may choose adoption in response to an unplanned or untimely pregnancy. The life situations that contribute to this difficult decision are as varied as the people themselves.

Rhonda was seventeen years old and a junior in high school when she found out she was pregnant. She was active in her local drama club, was planning to apply to college, and had recently broken up with the father of her unborn child. Although her parents would have supported her if she had wanted to parent the baby, Rhonda chose adoption so she could continue growing up herself and so her baby would have the kind of life she was not in a position to provide.

Kathleen and Ron, both thirty-two, had been married for seven years and had three children. Their relationship became very rocky when Ron started to feel the increasing pressure of having to financially support his family, and Kathleen began to feel removed from the world outside her home. Ron worked incessantly, Kathleen felt unfulfilled, and their communication deteriorated. Soon, Kathleen was pregnant with another man's child. Stunned and confused, the couple began marriage counseling and with the help of their therapist decided adoption would be their best choice.

Pauline was a single, thirty-six-year-old law student working part time in a law firm. She had taken some time off from her education, but was now committed to finishing school and taking the bar exam. She had never thought of herself as a mother, so when she discovered that her birth control had failed her, she was devastated and conflicted. After much thought, Pauline chose adoption because she knew of many families who desperately wanted to adopt. The father agreed with her decision and participated in the adoption plan, although the two of them were no longer in a relationship.

Stephanie was twenty-one years old and the single mother of Tiffany, a beautiful two-and-a-half-year-old girl. Stephanie did not receive any financial or emotional support from Tiffany's father, so she had been living on state assistance. She had hoped to return to trade school and become a respiratory therapist once Tiffany began kindergarten, so it was overwhelming to find out she was pregnant again. Her relationship with the father, Curtis, was new and tentative, so for financial and emotional reasons they decided to place their child for adoption.

Choosing adoption instead of abortion or parenting is a very personal choice. You may gather advice from friends and family and consult professionals, but ultimately the decision must be yours. No one really knows what it is like to be in your shoes, and no one really knows what is right for you.

Reasons for Choosing Adoption

One of the most common reasons for placing a child for adoption is feeling unprepared emotionally to parent a child at the time or under the circumstances. You might have personal dreams or goals that feel more pressing. You may wish to be in a committed relationship or married before starting or adding to your family. Some birthparents say they feel burdened by unresolved feelings from their own childhoods that they would like to explore and address before becoming parents.

"I was raised in a series of foster homes, with occasional visits from my mother. Her life was very chaotic, so I never knew what it was like to have a stable parent. I don't even know how to be a mother. I want something better for my baby."

Regina, 24-year-old birthmother

While some women may have the support and help of the birthfather to make a decision or follow through with an adoption plan, expectant mothers are often on their own. Facing the likelihood of being a single parent dissuades many women from parenting. This is especially true when expectant mothers already have one or more children. They know what it is like to be a single parent and feel overwhelmed at the prospect of caring for yet another child alone.

"I was already the single parent of a three-year-old, and I knew I couldn't raise two by myself. I felt like we would all be shortchanged: I would feel stressed and stretched way too thin, my daughter wouldn't get enough of me, and the baby wouldn't get what he needed either."

Christine, 34-year-old birthmother

Sometimes unplanned pregnancies occur in very new relationships. Other times the expectant mothers will use their own experiences as children or their parents' experiences to help them make their decision. For example, when Dianna became pregnant she and Rick had only been together for six months. Both felt their relationship was too unstable and new to commit to raising a child together, and neither felt comfortable with abortion. Dianna knew her mother and father had married when pregnant with her older brother, and she decided she wanted to begin her family feeling more prepared.

Sometimes an expectant mother knows she never really wanted to be a mother. She feels different from some of her friends who happily anticipate motherhood. She may have pursued a meaningful career while her friends were having babies. She may have a very full and satisfying life, with or without a partner, and not have planned on parenting.

In some communities, placing a child for adoption is a very unpopular, even taboo, choice. Some young women may not even know that adoption is a choice because it is never talked about in their community. Many young women facing an unplanned pregnancy are encouraged to have an abortion or to parent their babies. The pressure can come from their families, their peer groups, or their schools.

For these reasons, making an adoption plan can be a particularly difficult decision for a young woman. Most students attending teen parenting programs do not consider adoption, and often the curriculum does not present adoption as a legitimate option. And while abortion and teen parenting are widely discussed in the media as options, adoption is not. Accordingly, those who do think about making an adoption plan may feel hesitant to talk about it or worry that they would be unsupported if they explored it.

Young expectant mothers usually cite wanting to finish their education or not feeling that they are emotionally ready to parent as reasons for considering adoption. They may have seen friends who chose to parent struggle with the difficult realities of caring for a baby, and they want something different for their lives.

"In my PAPT (pregnant and parenting teen) program, I am the only one who placed my child for adoption. A lot of my friends said, 'How can you give up your child?' or they'd say, 'You made your bed, now lie in it!' but I knew I was doing the responsible

thing. I could see how they were having a hard time just getting by."

Meghan, 15-year-old birthmother

Unfortunately, the reaction this young woman received from her classmates is all too common. Instead of focusing on what may be in the best interest of the child and the expectant mother, the conversation focuses on making the expectant mother feel guilty if she does not choose to parent.

Sometimes young women chose adoption because the pregnancy is the result of a rape, incest or other violence. They hope the adoption will diminish their connection to the birthfather or the traumatic events that led to the pregnancy. Although adoption may be the right choice, painful and emotionally complicated circumstances such as these will require professional guidance and counseling if the expectant mother is to recover from the trauma that led to the pregnancy. It will also help her deal with the complicated emotions that an adoption is likely to bring up.

How Do I Know If Adoption Is Right for Me?

There are many reasons expectant mothers choose adoption over other options. How do you begin to explore whether it is the right choice for you? You can start by looking at your feelings the moment you found out you were pregnant.

"When I first found out, I was mortified. As soon as I walked out of the clinic after finding out I was too far along to terminate the pregnancy, adoption was the first word out of my mouth."

Latise, 18-year-old birthmother

"I was scared and excited at the same time. I was scared because I had no idea what to expect but also really excited about being pregnant and having a life growing inside of me. I kept asking myself, 'Am I parent material?' "

Joan, 18-year-old birthmother

If you are unsure about adoption, we encourage you to take time to consider all the options available to you. Each choice carries with it lifelong consequences, involving not only your future but also the future of your child. Rather than limiting your consideration to how the decision will affect your life right now, it is very helpful to imagine what your life will look like in the future with each of your options.

Choosing to Parent

Babies can be irresistibly adorable. A baby can look at you as if you were the most important and wonderful thing in her universe. If you have never been a mom, this is likely to be your image of parenting. If you are a parent, or even if you have little brothers and sisters, you know that parenting is so much more than receiving unconditional love. Parenting means that your desires, needs, and personal goals will never again be your first priority. Are you ready for this lifelong responsibility?

Talk to some new moms in order to get a realistic picture of what parenting an infant is really like. Better yet, spend a few days with them. Ask the parents of toddlers what they think has been the most rewarding and the most difficult part of parenting. Try to picture yourself doing these things with a baby.

Take time to reflect on what it felt like when you were a child. Think about the things you liked and didn't like about the way your parents raised you. What are your hopes and dreams for this child? Are you in a position to provide the kinds of experiences you believe will contribute to your child's healthy development?

Imagine what you will do to support yourself and your child. Ask yourself if you will work, stay at home, or go to school. Determine what your income will be and if this will cover your expenses, including the additional expenses of a new baby such as diapers, formula, and daycare if you need to work. If you will need public assistance, you will need to determine if you qualify and how to apply for it.

We encourage you to explore the option of parenting, even if you are leaning toward abortion or adoption. When we receive calls from women who have never had a baby before and they tell us firmly that they are one hundred percent sure adoption is right for them, we are immediately concerned. In very early pregnancy, the baby often does not seem real. As the pregnancy progresses and you begin to feel the baby growing and kicking, you might feel a rush of emotion. It is at this point that you might reconsider adoption.

Abortion

When Nicolette became pregnant at the age of seventeen, she never for a moment considered abortion. It went against her strict Christian upbringing, so even though she was unmarried, she chose to have her baby.

Finding herself pregnant again when her son was only two years old, she knew she could not parent two children as a single mom. Raising Sonny was just about more than she could take, with what little she received from welfare and without support from her family.

She chose adoption and placed her new baby with a loving family. It was only a year after that when she found herself pregnant once again. She had been proud of her adoption decision, but it had taken a tremendous emotional commitment on her part. She did not think she could do it again, and this time she chose abortion. She worried how she would feel about herself afterward, but she did not regret her decision and felt abortion was the best option for her.

If you are considering abortion, get a full examination, including a pregnancy test and a physical exam, to make sure you are pregnant and to determine how far along you are in your pregnancy. Each state has its own laws regarding how far into a pregnancy a woman can have an abortion. Additionally, an abortion may not be available in your region, or the cost may prohibit you from seeking one.

You may also want to find out if there are any legal barriers to seeking abortion. Some states require a 24-hour waiting period between a counseling session and the abortion procedure. Other states require a minor to notify or get the consent of her parents or custodial guardian before the procedure. In most cases, for a woman over the age of eighteen, the abortion decision is private and confidential and made between her and her health care provider.

If abortion is an option you are considering, we encourage you to take the time you need to explore your own feelings about this very important decision. Ask yourself:

- What are your and your family's beliefs about abortion?

- If your belief has always been that abortion is wrong, and now you find yourself considering it, are you giving yourself permission to fully explore this option?

- Do you have friends or family members who will support your decision to have an abortion regardless of their own views?

The issue of abortion is highly emotional and can cause volatile public debate. It is also a personal and private decision. Each woman experiences this decision and its aftermath differently. Some women say they felt incredibly sad while others say they experienced immediate relief from the burden of the unwanted pregnancy and were grateful to have had the choice. Some women have mixed feelings about this choice before and after an abortion, and need to restructure their previously held beliefs to heal in a healthy way.

Many health clinics provide free, professional, non-directive counseling to women regarding their choices when they have an unplanned pregnancy. Please be sure to go to a health clinic with non-directive counseling. Many "pregnancy crisis centers" are anti-abortion organizations that provide biased information about abortion. Planned Parenthood and similar organizations provide non-directive and unbiased information about abortion.

If You Are Seriously Considering Adoption

If you feel that adoption is the best choice, it is important to explore your emotions. Many women find that, while they believe their adoption decision is a good one for them and for their child, they have a difficult time facing up to the reality of the associated feelings.

Most women who chose adoption say they thought about it almost immediately when they learned they were pregnant, but did nothing to act on it until later in the pregnancy because they were still unsure. We have found that it is extremely helpful to explore your thoughts, feelings, and choices before proceeding with an adoption plan. In fact, most women do not move forward with an adoption plan until the last few months of pregnancy. By that time, abortion is no longer a practical option, and the only options are parenting or adoption.

The further along in the pregnancy you are, the more real the baby feels. You can feel the baby kicking and turning. Thoughts of parenting or placing the baby for adoption become more urgent and more real.

It might help to look at your previous experiences with loss and what your grief process was like. What did you find helpful and what might have hindered your healing process? How can you learn from these experiences to prepare for the grief involved in choosing adoption?

When they are able to envision the tough parts of an adoption decision, most women start the process of grieving and "letting go" which is essential to any adoption. Here are some things to think about when considering adoption:

- Picture yourself carrying a baby full-term but not taking that baby home with you from the hospital.

- How will it feel to step out of the role of "mother" and give that role to another person? Can you imagine someone other than yourself parenting your child?

- How might it feel to not be present for your child's first tooth, first steps, first day of school and other milestones?

- Imagine having given birth but not having the people in your life see you as a mother.

- How would you feel about having a connection to the child forever even though you would not be his or her parent?

- How will it feel to accept the identity of your child's birthparent? What does that role look like to you?

- If you are in a relationship with the birthfather, reflect on how you see your relationship after you place the baby for adoption.

How do you feel when you picture these scenarios? Acknowledging the difficulty of this decision will help you prepare for it and gather strength in the months ahead. In our experience, women who refused to look at their feelings or who denied there would be any difficulty often had the most painful post-adoption recovery. Even though your decision to place your child for adoption feels "right" to you, it does not mean you will not feel sad.

Sarah was a thirty-two-year-old graphic designer who felt pressured to decide how to handle her unplanned pregnancy. Her current boyfriend was not the father of her baby, and she felt compelled to hurry up and eliminate the tension in her new relationship. She chose to do an open adoption during her eighth week of pregnancy and had met and connected with a family before the end of her first trimester. Although she was happy with her decision to make an adoption plan, in retrospect, Sarah wished she had slowed down and taken more time to decide.

Even if you are due to deliver in one week, it is very important for you to be able to think about your decision for a while until you have truly "tried it on" and are sure that it fits.

"I wish someone had told me it wouldn't kill me just to sit with my feelings for a little while. I was so anxious that I thought just making a decision would feel better. It did for a while, but as the pregnancy progressed and I began to feel the baby move inside of me, I realized that in my rush to decide, I had avoided a lot of the feelings I had toward the baby."

Celia, 23-year-old birthmother

Who Chooses Open Adoption

As you explore placement, be mindful of any preconceived ideas you have about adoption or any stereotypes you have about what birthparents are like or about what kind of people place a child for adoption. This can be especially challenging if you have ideas based on movies, other people's experiences, or if foster parents raised you.

You may need to look at adoption in its modern "open" form. When secrecy was the hallmark of adoption, there was an inordinate amount of shame associated with the idea. Our culture often portrayed birthparents as "promiscuous" or "selfish," potential adoptive families as "barren," and adoptees as "unwanted." The truth is that birthparents and adoptive parents are selfless, courageous, loving people, and children in open adoptions are doubly wanted and doubly loved.

It is important to remember that your own unspoken or unconscious attitudes toward birthparents may influence your decision or affect the way you feel about yourself if you make an adoption plan. Remember that your experiences, feelings, thoughts, and circumstances are unique. It can be very helpful to solicit feedback from people you trust, but ultimately your values will be the most important ones to examine.

Is Adoption My Decision Alone?

The expectant mother is usually the primary decision maker regarding placing a child for adoption, but sometimes other people can prevent an adoption. The most important other person is the biological father of the child, whose rights may be equal to yours depending on your individual circumstances and the laws of the state where the baby is born. In addition, if you are married, separated, or recently divorced, your spouse or ex-spouse may have equal rights in the adoption decision, even if he or she is not the biological father of the baby. The courts will presume an ex-husband is the father unless you can convince them that he is not. A wife or ex-wife is not the biological parent, but as a legal or presumed parent they may have legal rights to the child (see Chapter 13 for additional information for Lesbian birthmothers).

If you or your child's father is Native American, the adoption may also be subject to the Indian Child Welfare Act (ICWA), which means the tribe or tribes involved must approve any adoption plan. It is important to disclose your or the birthfather's Native American heritage early in the process so that the adoption provider can notify the tribes involved. If a tribe deems the child eligible for enrollment, they will then make a determination to intervene or to allow the adoption to proceed.

In most states, you can make an adoption plan at the age of twelve or older without the consent of your parents. However, most young people under the age of eighteen prefer to involve their parents in their adoption decision. If you are under legal guardianship, you may have to get permission from your guardian.

The grandparents of the child (your parents or the birthfather's parents) do not have legal rights to block an adoption unless they have developed a significant relationship with the child or have parented the child for you. In this case, the grandparents may be able to get the court to give them the authority to care for the child. This will not be the situation if you are making an adoption plan while pregnant.

Telling the Birthfather

The father of the baby has important rights in the adoption process. Individual state laws and his level of involvement will affect his legal standing. This means that if you want to pursue adoption and the father objects or contests, you may not be able to place your child for adoption. It is important to let the father of the baby know early on about the pregnancy and your interest in adoption.

If you are unsure of how to broach the subject with the father, you can ask your adoption professional for guidance. Alternatively, if you would rather not have any direct interaction with the father, you can ask the adoption professional to handle this communication for you. Overall, we have found that most men in this position will agree with an adoption plan when they are included in the decision-making process. For several reasons, hiding your adoption plans from the birthfather can result in negative outcomes later.

The most important reason for including the birthfather is that he has a right to know about a child he has fathered. Second, if you are seriously considering adoption, his cooperation and emotional support may be helpful. Finally, your child may want to know the medical, social, and cultural history of his or her biological father.

In most states, the courts may not finalize the adoption without confirming that the father is aware of it. If you knowingly keep your pregnancy and adoption plans from the legal father of the baby, he can challenge the adoption and may even be able to overturn it. Most states require you to name the birthfather regardless of his involvement in your life. However, depending on circumstance, at the time of publication of this edition expectant mothers might not be required to do so in New York, Indiana, Georgia or Florida. However, even when it is not required, it is usually in the best interest of your child for the birthfather to know about the placement.

There are different criteria that determine the legal father of a child. If you are married, separated, or very recently divorced, your husband (or ex-husband) is legally the father of your baby, whether or not he is the biological father. This is a common occurrence, and an expectant mother in these situations must notify the biological father and also get the consent of her husband or ex-husband.

If your husband or ex-husband is not the biological father, you can sometimes convince a judge that you do not need his consent to the adoption. Your proof that he could not be the father must be overwhelming, such as, he was in prison or deployed out of the country with the military around the time of conception.

While paternity can be determined prenatally through a blood test of the expectant mother and the possible biological father, at the time of publication of this book it is too expensive for most families to consider. (We expect that over time the price will come down.) A paternity test after the baby is born is much less expensive, but generally requires a mouth swab from the mother, father and child. Sometimes, but not always, paternity can be determined with a mouth swab from just the father and child.

In many states the biological father's rights may be equal to yours, even if you are not married to him, and you may need to get his consent to the adoption. Most adoption practitioners treat all potential fathers as if they are the legal fathers and have equal rights to the child. This is a legal issue so we suggest you consult an adoption attorney about the birthfather's rights in your case.

If you had intercourse with more than one partner around the time of conception, the adoption professional will need to address the rights of each partner unless you have a prenatal DNA test to determine the father. You should confide in your adoption counselor if there is more than one possible father. This situation is more common than you might expect, and it is important that all possible birthfathers be notified and consent to termination of their parental rights in order to ensure the completion of the adoptive placement.

Telling Family and Friends

It is a personal decision whether or not you tell family or friends about your pregnancy and interest or intentions regarding adoption. In most cases, you have no legal obligation to share this information with your family.

However, if you are a minor and live at home with your parents, you have a very different responsibility to your family than if you are an adult woman living on your own and supporting yourself. If you are a minor, you should ask an attorney or agency representative about the laws in your particular state. Some states require an adult guardian to represent a minor expectant mother when she signs the paperwork terminating her legal rights to the child. Most states allow minors older than twelve years to make an adoption plan without the consent of a parent or guardian, but we encourage minors to involve their parents or guardians in the decision.

If you are seriously considering adoption, we encourage you to confide in close friends or family members who can help you sort through your situation. You should also confide in those whose opinion might significantly influence your decision should they find out about your pregnancy. All too often we have worked with women, particularly young women, who intended to keep the pregnancy and adoption a secret and then changed their minds about an adoptive placement when their family found out. This can be tragic for all concerned when it occurs after making an adoption plan, choosing the adoptive family, and placing the baby. In other instances, expectant mothers have been surprised by how supportive their family was, and they regretted missing out on the support they would have received if they had confided in their family about the pregnancy and adoption plan.

Depending on your circumstance, telling your family about the pregnancy might be intimidating. Some expectant women make an adoption plan simply to avoid this confrontation altogether. However, even though your family's reactions may be difficult to deal with, their anger will ultimately subside. If the overriding reason for making an adoption plan is to avoid telling your family about the pregnancy, you are using a permanent solution to solve a temporary problem.

Alternatively, if you know that adoption is the right decision for you and your child, explaining your situation once you have researched adoption may help the conversation move in a constructive direction. If you are reasonably certain an adoption is what you want, and you think your family will try to talk you out of it, find a trusted friend, counselor, teacher, or clergyperson who can come with you to talk to your family.

Your family may not immediately embrace your plans. While you have had days, weeks, or even months to acknowledge and accept your pregnancy, your family will be hearing about it for the first time. Remember the rush of emotions you felt when you first found out you were pregnant? They will have a lot to think about too, so give them a little breathing space. They may feel they are losing a child if you choose adoption, so try to be patient with their grieving process.

If you are thinking about open adoption, keep in mind that this may be a new concept to your family. Birth grandparents may be more comfortable with and even supportive of their son or daughter's adoption decision if they know that they may be able to meet the adopting parents and have an ongoing relationship with them and the child.

Financial Support and Living Accommodations

Some women need financial support during their pregnancy including options for living accommodations. Most states will provide expectant mothers with direct or indirect support for pregnancy-related expenses, but the extent of this support varies widely. In some states, expectant mothers can only receive support for the pregnancy-related health care for them and their babies, but only if an agency acts as the financial intermediary for these reimbursements.

Other states allow not only pregnancy-related health care but living expenses and other related support as well. All states that allow prospective birthmothers to receive support require that the assistance be directly related to the pregnancy and adoption. Any payments not directly linked to the pregnancy or legitimate adoption costs could be misconstrued as a payment in return for the child, which is illegal.

Before you make any financial arrangements regarding support during your pregnancy or after, we recommend you consult with an adoption agency or with an attorney familiar with adoption practice in your state and in the state of the adopting family.

Just How Sure Do I Have to Be?

Throughout your pregnancy and even beyond it is normal to waver back and forth when deciding if adoption is the right choice. Many women have reported they were waiting for the time they felt "one hundred percent sure" of their decision. For some birthparents, this is realistic, but for others, "surety" is more fluid.

Part of this process may involve acknowledging that you actually have conflicting feelings about the pregnancy, the baby, or how to proceed. This does not necessarily mean that you have made the wrong choice or that you will change your mind. It simply means that choosing adoption is a very difficult and complicated decision that, by its very nature, involves some level of ambiguity.

CHAPTER 2: CHOOSING THE RIGHT ADOPTION FOR YOU

How to Decide on the Right Adoption Plan for You

The spectrum of adoption practice has changed dramatically in recent decades. Traditional closed adoptions have shrunk to a tiny minority of about five percent. About forty percent of adoptions have semi-open arrangements where the adoption professional sends the birthmother updates on how the child is doing. Another fifty-five percent of adoptions have a fully open arrangement. [1]

According to the same report, women who place their infants in fully open adoptions report less grief, regret and worry, as well as greater peace of mind than those who do not have direct contact with their children.

"For me, it really made a difference in whether or not I would place my son for adoption—knowing where he was going and who his parents were going to be helped me feel safe."

Heather, 19-year-old birthmother

---

[1] "Openness in Adoption: From Secrecy and Stigma to Knowledge and Connections" - Authors: Deborah H. Siegel, Ph.D. and Susan Livingston Smith, LCSW (Evan B. Donaldson Adoption Institute, 2012)

"Even though I knew my decision was right, I just couldn't bring myself to get involved with selecting and meeting the parents. I really trusted my adoption counselors to tell me everything I wanted to know, but I just had to keep my mind on getting back to my life. I like that I have the option to find out how my child is doing later on, when I am more ready. That feels good, but for right now, it is just too hard."

Ashley, 21-year-old birthmother

Closed Adoption

In a truly closed adoption, neither the birthparents nor the adopting parents receive any identifying information about one another. Typically, a social worker and an adoption agency chose the adoptive family, and the expectant mother does not participate in the process. In some cases, the agency will ask the expectant mother what her wishes for a family are, and the social worker may consider those wishes when selecting an adoptive family.

The social worker or adoption agency does not provide the adoptive family with any information about the birth family except for the health, medical, or social history required by law. Most people adopted in this country before the 1980s were not given complete and accurate medical information about their birth families. Many must now go through lengthy legal procedures or costly investigative searches to obtain information about their origins.

In most states, legislation passed in the mid-twentieth century sealed adoption records, only allowing a judge to open them in special circumstances, such as a medical emergency or when the adoptee reaches legal age (usually eighteen) and all parties agree. Many birthparents are, to this day, unable to find out about the children they placed for adoption years ago. In response, adoptee activists and their supporters started an "open records" movement that has forced many, although not all, states to open their adoption records allowing adoptees and birth families to contact one another.

Open Adoption

The hallmark of open adoption is full sharing of information between the birth and adoptive family and ongoing contact between the child and the birth family. The information available to the birthparents includes pictures of the adoptive family, their full names, ages, place of residence, marital or relationship status, whether or not they have other children, and so forth.

Expectant mothers have the opportunity to review letters and online profiles of prospective parents until they find ones they would like to meet. Upon meeting, both parties gather additional information about one another and can ask questions about their wishes for ongoing contact to determine if their expectations are compatible. Usually the birth and adoptive families continue to stay in touch long after the adoption is completed, and many birth and adoptive families view each other as "extended family."

With the help of your adoption professional, details of any future contact are determined before the placement. Arrangements for parties who live within driving distance from each other usually include a few visits the first year, and annual visits thereafter. If visiting requires a long plane ride, it is more common to plan for annual visits over a long weekend. Additionally, emails, pictures, phone calls and video chats are often incorporated into the contracts for continued contact.

"I was scared about how I might feel, seeing my baby with her new parents in their home for the first time. I didn't know if I would be jealous, or if I would just want to take her home with me, or what. But it really helped. I saw how much her parents loved her, and I could picture what her life was going to be like. It's what I wanted for her. I knew that day I had made the right decision."

Patti, 26-year-old birthmother

Some early critics of open adoption expressed concern the birthmother would not be able to handle the ongoing relationship with her child and that openness would make separation more

25

difficult. There is now significant research that shows birthparents generally have fewer problems when they participate in open adoptions. In the majority of open adoptions in which we are involved, the birthmother is able to heal more easily because she can see that the child is safe and happy and that the adopting parents love the child as their own.

A common fear of expectant women planning an adoption is that their children will grow up thinking that their birthmothers did not love them. However, in open adoption, birthmothers have the opportunity to show their children how much they love them. A birthmother's presence in her child's life inherently shows the child that she cares.

Many women are concerned that maintaining a presence in their children's lives will confuse the child as to who is the parent. But longitudinal studies have shown the opposite. Children who have a relationship with their birthmothers have a concrete understanding of everyone's role and, thus, are less confused than children in closed adoptions.

Children in open adoptions usually refer to their birthparents by their first names. Since they have always seen their birthmother as a relative and their adoptive parent(s) as their parent(s), that dynamic feels very normal to them. In fact, to a child in an open adoption, the idea of *not* knowing his or her birthparents would seem like a strange concept. In addition, research shows that adoptive parents in open adoptions do not find the relationship unusual or strange either, but rather a welcome addition to their extended family.

"The adoptive family has become like family to me. We talk or e-mail one to two times each month. They send pictures of "our daughter" at every stage. I send letters and cards at least once a month. The adoptive family has eased my fears by letting me set the pace and always letting me know what a gift I've given them. We get together a few times a year. I have given my daughter a wonderful life with everything she could want. And I know that I

found the perfect mom and dad for her because they love her just like I do."

Ashleigh, 19-year-old birthmother

Semi-Open or Mediated Adoption

Although today the vast majority of adoptions are open, some agencies, facilitators, and attorneys promote what they call semi-open or mediated adoptions. This type of adoption borrows from closed and open adoption in that the birth and adoptive families may meet and even share information about their families, but most contact is controlled and coordinated through the adoption agency, attorney or facilitator.

The attorney, facilitator, or agency does not disclose identifying information, such as addresses, last names, and phone numbers, and, while the birthmother receives updates through letters and pictures, there is no direct contact. The adoption professional coordinates all exchanges.

Many people who choose semi-open adoption eventually "open up" the adoption on their own by sharing information directly with one another without agency, facilitator, or attorney mediation. The adoptive parents have no legal obligation to agree to increased contact, but if the two families are comfortable with each other, they can proceed on their own.

Choosing the Right Adoption for You and Your Child

Now that you know what options are available, you may already know which type of adoption fits you best. At first, some women may be unsure about whether or not they want an open adoption. An unplanned pregnancy is very stressful, and the decision to place a child for adoption is usually very difficult. At this point, some women feel it would be a relief if someone else made the decisions for them. Others feel they do not have the skills or intuition to pick suitable parents. Still others fear contact with the family or the child will be too difficult for them emotionally or fear the responsibility of developing a relationship with an adopting family.

We have found that most women who initially choose a closed adoption will decide sometime later in the process that they want more participation. For example, they may want to hear more about the adoptive family, see a picture of the child, or meet the family. They also may realize later in life that they would like to know about the child.

If you are considering a closed or semi-open adoption, we encourage you to select an adoption professional who can offer you greater openness should you change your mind at any point along the way. You can do this either through a supportive agency or with an adoption attorney or adoption facilitator who supports openness in adoption.

Agency Adoption

An adoption agency may be either a public (state or county) or private (secular or religious) organization that is licensed to approve prospective parents for the purpose of adoption. An agency also places babies or children with those parents if the birthparents chose adoption.

Private adoption agencies are counseling-focused and provide support services before and after the child is born. Counselors work with birthparents through the grief and healing process, and many agencies offer lifetime counseling to birthparents free of charge. Agencies also tend to place more emphasis on educating adoptive parents and birthparents on the benefits of incorporating at least some level of openness into the adoption arrangement.

Each agency has its own protocol governing how much the prospective birthparents can participate in the adoption process. In an agency adoption, the adopting parents are pre-approved through an investigative process called a home study. As a result, prospective birthparents can be assured that the adoptive parents they select have already been through a thorough approval process that includes background checks, home inspections, employment verification and personal interviews (see "Elements of a Home Study," Chapter 3).

Sometimes prospective birthmothers and adoptive parents find each other on their own and then work with an agency to complete the adoption. These adoptions are still considered agency adoptions, and the agency will require the prospective adoptive parents to complete a home study before the placement.

Most secular agencies, like the IAC, provide non-directive counseling with information about parenting, abortion, and adoption. This allows potential birthparents to consider all the options. Many religious adoption agencies provide no information or only negative information about abortion.

For most states, in an agency adoption the birthmother signs papers terminating her parental rights after the baby is born. In some states, you sign the paperwork prior to the birth, but it is not final until a court terminates your rights after the birth. Most agencies will have the hospital release the baby to the adoptive parents' care, but some agencies place the baby in an interim care home until the birthmother's rights are terminated.

In most, but not all, states the timeframe for signing the termination papers is flexible, but the majority of birthparents choose to sign within two weeks of the birth. Each state has a different law regarding how many days, if any, a birthmother has to change her mind or revoke the termination of her parental rights.

Most agencies provide "designated adoption" paperwork, which allows the birthmother to name the potential adoptive parent(s) on the paperwork that terminates her parental rights. This requires the adoption agency to place the child with the specified family. If you want an open adoption, it is important to sign designated adoption paperwork that terminates your parental rights so that you know the name of the family that adopts your child.

Independent or Attorney Adoptions

Most, but not all, states allow independent or attorney adoptions. In every state that permits attorney adoptions, the adopting parents will be required to submit to a home study by a social worker before the finalization of the adoption. Most states require the state or a private adoption agency to employ the social workers that complete the home studies, but some states will allow self-employed social workers to provide home study services. In attorney adoptions, the social worker often does not complete the home study until after placement of the baby with the adoptive family. A home study assesses if a family is safe for a child, both physically and emotionally. (Chapter 3 has a detailed discussion of home studies)

In some states, attorneys must hire social workers to advise you of your rights before you sign the adoption paperwork terminating your parental rights. Some states require that you have an attorney representing you who is not also representing the potential adoptive parents, but in every state you have the right to ask for legal representation that is different from the attorney representing the potential adoptive family. Some adoption attorneys offer semi-open adoptions, but many also work with families who are seeking fully open adoptions, as well.

Adoption Facilitators

Adoption facilitators often advertise themselves as "adoption services." Potential adoptive families hire them to find prospective birthmothers, and they can offer you a selection of adoptive parents to choose from. But these professionals are neither agencies nor attorneys, and they cannot provide the counseling or legal services required for the adoption placement process. Facilitators are illegal in many states, so be sure you check the laws in your state before deciding to work with one.

If you work with a facilitator, you will need an adoption agency or an attorney to complete the adoption, including processing the termination of your parental rights and the finalization of the adoption. The facilitator will be able to recommend professionals for these services.

Selecting an Adoption Provider

Many women who decide to place a child for adoption start by going online and looking at the thousands of adoptive parent profiles posted on hundreds of websites. Although this may work for you, we recommend that you engage an adoption professional with an objective point of view who can advise you of your rights, help you evaluate if a potential adoptive family is a good fit, give you emotional support through the ups and downs, and advocate for you.

There are many ways to find the right program for you. You can ask your doctor, family lawyer, social worker, local social service agency, nurses at the hospital, family planning clinic, school nurse, counselor, or member of the clergy. Many of these professionals have had experience with local adoption providers and can recommend a good program. You can also research adoption providers online.

Keep in mind that the belief system of the adoption provider representing the family often drives the level of future contact that the prospective adoptive parents will agree to. If the provider does not have an option to do a fully open adoption, this may not be the best course to pursue. Even if you do not currently want an open adoption, you may want it in the future, so it is in your best interest to match with a family who would not close this option off.

Call for Information

Even though you can tell a lot from an adoption provider's web site, it is very important to call the agency, facilitator, or attorney. Before you call, make a list of questions that are important to you and leave a space to write down the provider's answers and your general impressions. You will begin to get an idea about the philosophy and services of each provider, as well as their general character. This will allow you to get a feel as to whether or not this provider is a good fit for you.

You should find an organization that believes in your right to make decisions about how you would like your adoption to proceed. You should also find a place that will advocate for and support you through this process from beginning to end.

Sample Questions for an Adoption Agency, Attorney, or Facilitator

- What type of adoptions do they typically facilitate? How do they define open adoption?

- What is the range of openness that they offer?

- Do they pre-select families or can you choose from all of their families who are open to your circumstance?

- Will the future contact agreement be legally enforceable?

- Can you choose the parents yourself?

- Do they have any restrictions on the type of families you can choose? For example, do they have single parents or gay, lesbian or transgender families? Can you choose a family of a different ethnicity?

- Do they provide counseling? If so, how long after the birth can you receive counseling?

- How soon after the birth or the placement must you sign paperwork to terminate your parental rights?

- When will your decision become irrevocable?

- Can you place your baby directly with a potential adoptive family or will your baby have to go into an interim care placement first?

- Can you place your baby with a family who lives in a different state?

- What expenses will your state allow the potential adoptive family to provide (e.g. counseling, medical expenses, living expenses)?

- What is the parental rights termination process for the birthfather?

- Do they have a birthparent support group or other birthparents with whom you can speak?

If You Cannot Find an Open Adoption Practitioner in Your Area

Almost every state has an open adoption practitioner. If you cannot find an open adoption provider in your state, you can work with an agency in another state, including national open adoption agencies like the IAC.

CHAPTER 3: FINDING THE RIGHT ADOPTIVE FAMILY FOR YOUR CHILD

After making the decision to place your child for adoption, the most important choice you will have to make is selecting the parents. Most expectant mothers approach the decision with a mixture of nervousness, sadness, and excitement. Some women report that they felt a lot of pressure to make the right decision. It can be scary to make such an important decision. It can also be a relief to finally have someone with whom to share your experience, someone who will find something joyous and wonderful about your pregnancy.

Still, most expectant mothers have numerous concerns about the prospective adoptive family: How will I know if these people will truly love my child? How can I be sure they will not abuse my child? What if I choose them and then find out they are not really who I thought they were? What if the adoptive family I choose will not let me see my child? How will I know they are the right parents for my child?

These are the typical questions with which most birthparents struggle and can be topics to discuss with your counselor. They are also good questions to ask yourself before choosing the adoptive family for your child. In addition, you must ask yourself other questions as you consider this choice: Can I accept that anyone I choose will have human faults? Can I let go of my worry and doubt once I have selected them? Can I trust that this family will love and raise my child to the best of their ability?

Getting Support from the Biological Father

For legal and ethical reasons, it is important that someone tell the father of your baby about the pregnancy and your desire to place the baby for adoption. Even though the idea of telling him may be intimidating, as long as the legal requirements for notification are met there are only certain circumstances that would allow him to stop the adoption. Every state has different laws and practices regarding the rights of the biological father. An adoption expert—an agency or attorney—can explain what the father's legal rights are in your state.

Although we support notifying biological fathers about an adoption so that the child may have access to his medical, social and cultural history, it is important to note that at the time of publication of this book at least four states, New York, Indiana, Georgia and Florida, do not require expectant mothers to disclose this information in most circumstances. Most states, however, do require you to notify the biological father about an adoption plan.

If you are not involved with the birthfather anymore and do not want to have direct contact with him, you can ask your adoption professional to inform him and handle any further communication. There is no legal requirement for you to have direct interaction with the birthfather.

Some expectant mothers do not experience problems involving the biological father. If you and the biological father can reach an agreement about adoption, you may feel more confident and supported in your decision. Regardless of their current relationship with the birthfather, some expectant mothers have told us that having his support was important.

Even if the birthfather is initially unsupportive of your adoption plans, there is a good chance that he will become less resistant after your adoption professional counsels him. If he was not involved in making the plan, it is common for a birthfather to reject the idea of adoption, even if he is not involved during the pregnancy. The birthfather often feels that he should have been consulted before anyone took steps to proceed with an adoption plan.

In these cases, an adoption professional can address his feelings and educate him on all of the aspects of current adoption practice. Additionally, if you are choosing an open adoption where the birthfather can have ongoing contact with the child and the adoptive family, he may be more amenable to the adoption plan.

Some expectant mothers do not want to tell the biological father about the pregnancy or the adoption plans. Perhaps there was violence in the relationship or the pregnancy resulted from rape or a coercive sexual encounter. In these situations, each state has its own threshold regarding requirements to inform the birthfather. Your counselor can help you sort through your emotions while protecting your legal rights, and ensuring your safety.

Most often the expectant mother is reluctant to involve the biological father because she does not want him to be part of her life anymore or because she fears he will not consent to the adoption. It is important for the child, though, that someone notify the biological father. The child will eventually need access to the medical and cultural history of his or her biological father. In addition, some adoptions cannot proceed, or can be overturned by a judge, if no one notifies the biological father. This would be a tragedy for your child.

It is far better to find out now whether or not the biological father will consent to the adoption, and work with your adoption professional to plan accordingly. Finally, as noted above, the overwhelming reason someone should notify the biological father is so the child will have complete information regarding his or her history and know that his or her biological father was part of the process.

We recommend that you welcome the biological father into the decision-making and adoption planning processes, if possible. If you are unwilling or unable to notify the biological father on your own to tell him about the pregnancy and adoption plan, your adoption facilitator, counselor, case worker, or attorney can help you by making the call or writing to him.

In most, though not all, cases we believe the best approach is personal and direct contact from you. If you are nervous about this, ask the biological father to come with you to a counseling session so that your counselor can help you and him adjust to the situation together.

If You Are Not Sure Who the Birthfather Is

Many expectant mothers feel ashamed to admit they are not entirely sure who is the father of their baby, but this is a far more common situation then you might imagine. It is in the best interest of your child to talk honestly with your counselor about the situation. That way the counselor can make sure you only receive information about the prospective parents who would be best suited for the child regardless of the father's race or health background. Most prospective adoptive families will understand and will not judge you negatively because of this situation. It will also be important for the security of your child's adoption that the adoption provider terminates the parental rights of all potential and unknown biological fathers.

The Race and Ethnicity of the Child and of the Adoptive Parents

All adoption providers ask prospective adoptive families what race and ethnicity of child they would be interested in adopting. Federal law allows parents to adopt a child of a different race, particularly when the expectant parents choose the family and approve of the placement.

If you are considering placing your child in a family that does not share your child's racial or ethnic background, it is acceptable (and important) to ask the prospective adopting parents about their feelings on and plans for raising a child who does not share their race or ethnicity.

Many agencies require adoptive families who are interested in transracial adoption to take a training course that explores the issues they may face as a multi-racial family, including how their child may experience growing up in a family that does not share his or her racial and/or ethnic identity. The course will help prospective parents process their feelings regarding ethnic and cultural heritage before making this decision. It will also guide them in considering their community's openness to transracial families and how they might incorporate their child's cultural background into their family. Finally there is an extensive discussion of the importance of talking about race and racism in transracial families, and the harm that can result if this topic is ignored or downplayed.

Questions to Ask Adopting Parents of Another Race and/or Ethnicity

- Why did you decide to adopt a child of this particular race/ethnicity?

- How do you think you can help your child with issues related to racism or white privilege?

- What sort of things do you feel you can do to help this child deal with the fact that he or she is of a different race and/or ethnicity than you?

- Do you have any friends or family who are of the same race and/or ethnicity as the child?

- Do you live in a neighborhood where people who share this child's race and/or ethnicity also reside?

- How do you plan to ensure that this child will feel proud of his or her race and/or ethnicity?

- How will you connect your child to people who share his or her racial and/or ethnic heritage?

- Are you interested in and willing to stay in touch with the birthparents with whom the child shares his or her racial and/or ethnic identity?

- How are you intending to stay connected to an adoption community that supports and provides education for transracial families?

- Do you plan to adopt other children? If so, will you adopt transracially?

- How would your family and friends relate to a child of a different ethnicity?

- How would you feel if you adopted a biracial child with whom you share some racial background and he or she ended up looking more like the race you do not have in common?

- How will you feel if others perceive you as a "different" family?

There are no right or wrong answers to these questions, but the answers and ensuing discussion might give you insight into how a particular family might deal with the challenges of parenting in a transracial family.

Birthparents of Native American (American Indian) or Alaskan Native Heritage

Tell your counselor right away if you or the biological father has (or may have) Native American or Alaskan[2] Native ancestry. Due to the Indian Child Welfare Act (ICWA) there may be restrictions on your adoption planning, especially if you or close family members are registered members of a tribe. Congress passed the ICWA to protect Native American and Alaskan Native

---

[2] Inuit, Yapik, Aleut and other indigenous Alaskans

children whom state social workers were removing and placing in non-Native homes.

In these cases, the adoption counselor will contact the appropriate tribe or tribes to make sure they will allow the adoption. If you do not know the name of the tribe or tribes from which you may be descended, the adoption counselor will contact the Federal Bureau of Indian Affairs to determine if you are on their list of tribal members.

Depending on your situation, the tribe may have jurisdiction over the adoptive placement of the child. Some tribes will insist that other tribal members adopt the child. Other tribes will allow the adoption but insist that an open adoption agreement include regular contact with the tribe, such as attending a yearly tribal gathering or powwow. Still other tribes will claim the child as a member of the tribe, but allow the adoption to continue without any other restrictions.

There is no way to know what a tribe will do until you or the counselor contacts them and they confirm their decision in writing. It is vitally important that the adoption counselor completes the tribal notification correctly, as any mistakes can overturn an adoption, even years later.

Drugs, Alcohol, and Smoking

If you used drugs or alcohol before or during your pregnancy, talk with your adoption counselor. You should also let your counselor know if you smoke cigarettes or are taking any prescription medications. People often feel ashamed or guilty in disclosing this information, but your counselor will understand.

One of the most important reasons to be honest is to ensure that the adoptive families you choose will understand and accept this information. No matter what your circumstances, there is always an appropriate family available who will want to adopt your child. Providing honest information allows them to make an informed decision.

It is extremely difficult for a prospective adoptive family to learn about drug and alcohol usage later on. It damages the trust in the relationship and can even disrupt the match if your substance use falls outside their comfort level.

Selecting the Adoptive Family

Today it is possible to go online and see every prospective potential adoptive parent in the country. Every adoption agency, facilitator, and attorney posts online profiles of their prospective adoptive families. In addition, there are many additional sites listing adoptive families that are not affiliated with any adoption provider.

In fact, it is common for birthparents to find several adoptive families that they like on the Internet, and each of these families may be working with several different adoption providers. If you can determine the adoption professional the prospective adoptive family is working with, it is important to investigate and perhaps call the adoption professional using the questions we suggested in Chapter Two before contacting the family directly. Remember most prospective adoptive families will be taking their cues about adoption, particularly open adoption, from the adoption professional with whom they have chosen to work.

If you cannot determine the adoption professional the family has chosen to work with, or you would rather talk to a family before talking to an adoption professional it is important to call them to see if you feel a connection. Although email can start the conversation, it is always a good idea to speak to them as well, since a single phone call often provides more information than numerous email or text messages.

It can be scary to talk on the phone, but we really encourage you to do so as it is often the best way to evaluate if a prospective adoptive family is a good fit for you. If you choose this approach, please be aware that some families will not be completely candid with you. For example, the adoptive family may have decided they only want to consider adopting children of a particular racial or ethnic background. This is not information that most families are comfortable sharing, so you may not find out this type of information until you are in contact with their adoption provider.

Some potential birthparents become overwhelmed after looking at a dozen, or hundreds, or sometimes thousands of potential adoptive parent profiles online. They decide to work with an adoption provider to help them select families that are open to their situation.

All adoption programs have different policies for selecting the potential adoptive family. Some programs give you a choice of all the prospective parents they currently have waiting in their program, and others choose several families they believe would be appropriate for you.

When potential adoptive families join an adoption program, the provider asks them to define the parameters of the situations they are open to considering. Factors such as the race and health of the birthparents, the potential prenatal exposure of the child to drugs, alcohol, or smoking, and possible additional costs, such as helping you with living expenses, are important in determining a feasible match.

For example, if a family has indicated they are only willing to adopt a child born to two African American birthparents, and you or the birthfather are not African American, it will not be a good match. If you have used drugs or alcohol at any time during the pregnancy and a certain family in the program has indicated they are not willing to adopt a child exposed to those substances, then they are not the right family for you or your child.

It is very important for you, the expectant mother, to be honest with the adoption counselor about your situation before you start the process of selecting parents for your child. Once the professional gathers this information, she will be able to identify how many of the waiting families fit your profile.

If you decide that you would like a larger selection than one professional can provide, you can continue your search by contacting additional adoption providers. You have a right to research as many professionals and prospective families as you like. This is an extremely important decision, and the level of confidence you have in your choice of prospective parents will directly affect your ability to go through with the placement.

Some programs offer information, including photographs, about the prospective parents without including any identifying information, such as their last names. Please be cautious in these situations because if you place your child with a family and do not have any identifying information, even if you meet them in person, you may not be able to find them later. Even if you feel that you do not want contact right way, it is prudent to allow yourself this option if you change your mind months or years later.

Getting More Information about the Prospective Adoptive Family

You might want more information about a prospective adoptive family than is initially provided. It is your right to ask for as much information as you need in order to make a good decision. If you are working with a licensed agency, they will have completed a home study on the prospective family, which will include information such as marital status; if married, how long they have been married, previous marriages, other children, religion, their home environment, child discipline beliefs, whether or not they smoke, and any history of alcohol or drug abuse.

Beware of any person, organization, or agency that does not allow you to have this information. While most agencies will not simply hand over their confidential files to you, just as you would not expect them to release your confidential information to any adopting parent, they should be able to provide you with basic information and a summary of the home study findings. At many agencies, prospective adoptive parents sign a release that allows the agency to share the home study with a birthparent who is interested in matching with the family.

Elements of a Home Study

1. Background Check:

- Criminal record clearance
- Child abuse index clearance
- Out-of-state child abuse/neglect clearances (Adam Walsh Act)

2. Motivations and Readiness to Adopt:

- Why does this family want to adopt?
- Is it a good time to add a child to the family, emotionally and financially?

3. Relationship/Marriage Assessment:

- Previous marriages
- For couples:
    o Length and stability of marriage or relationship
    o How do they deal with differences?

4. Family History:

- Upbringing: childhood, adolescence, and adulthood
- Relationships with parents and siblings, past and present
- Medical and mental health assessments

5. Child Rearing Experiences:

- How were they raised/disciplined?
- How do they plan to discipline?
- Experience with children
- Child-care plans

6. Finances:

- Job security and satisfaction
- Income and assets

7. Type of Child Desired:

- Age, race, ethnicity, disabilities
- Social worker's assessment of their strengths and limitations regarding parenting

8. Adoption Issues:

- How much openness do they want in an adoption?
- Feelings toward birthparents
- Reading and workshops taken to prepare for adoption

9. Religion:

- Religious/spiritual upbringing, if any
- Current spiritual beliefs and practices, if any
- In what religious and/or spiritual tradition, if any, will the family raise the child?

10. Goals and Hobbies:

- Educational values and aspirations for a child
- Travel plans, career goals, and personal goals

11. Home and Community Inspection:

- Home visit (all family members interviewed)
- Assessment of overall neighborhood
- Home inspection for health and safety

12. Assessment:

- Three or four letters of reference
- Social worker's general assessment of the family's ability to parent an adopted child

Other Selection Criteria

Some birthparents select a prospective adoptive family based on a "gut feeling." Other birthparents have very specific things they are looking for in parents for their child, such as their religious beliefs or lack thereof, how they plan to discipline the child, whether the child will be in child care, and so forth.

While it can be helpful to have a picture in your mind, we encourage you to be open and flexible when considering families. If you have some "absolutes" then you should discuss those with your adoption counselor. However, it is important to let your counselor know the difference between your absolutes and your wish list.

Age

Many adopting parents are in their thirties or forties. This is often the age when heterosexual and lesbian families decide they want children and subsequently discover that they have fertility problems. Nevertheless, some adopting parents are in their twenties, and some are in their sixties. While age can tell you something about the person, it is not a predictor of the quality of the parenting. Good parenting comes at all ages.

Religion or Spiritual Beliefs

For some expectant mothers, religion is very important. Sometimes expectant mothers will tell us, "I only want to consider Jewish families" or "I do not want my child brought up in any organized religion." There are adopting families of every religious belief, including Buddhist, Christian, Hindu, Jewish, Muslim, Wiccan and many others. In addition, some adopting families are not religious at all or consider themselves "spiritual" but do not identify with any religious tradition.

Families With or Without Children

Sometimes expectant mothers make a selection based on whether or not the family already has children. Expectant mothers who choose adoptive parents without other children may like the idea because they believe that the family will be especially excited, that the child will get undivided attention, or because they want to choose a family that has not yet been able to experience parenthood.

Other expectant mothers prefer a family that already has children. They may want to be sure their child will have a sibling, or they believe they can get a sense of how the family parents by watching them with their other children. In addition, if the family adopted their other child, the expectant mother can see for herself how comfortable the family is with adoption or ongoing contact with birthparents.

Working Parents and Stay-at-Home Parents

Many adopting families cannot afford to stay home with their children full-time, but there are some who have made plans to ensure that one parent will be home full-time with the child. Some adopting families, however, have arranged to take extended time off from work after an adoption. Others have jobs that are flexible enough to work around caring for a new baby.

Single Parents

We see more and more single men and women who decide to parent without a partner. Many of these men and women have extended families and a large circle of close friends who will help them create the type of family they feel is important for raising a child.

Do not assume that a single parent cannot be a full-time parent to the child. Some single parents have either financial or family resources that make it possible for them to stay home and raise the child. Alternatively, they may have a relative who will be helping with childcare. Remember that it is in your best interest to keep an open mind as you move through the selection process.

Adoptive Families with Medical Conditions or Disabilities

A prospective adoptive parent or their child may have medical conditions or a disability. Disabilities can include obvious ones, like being blind, deaf or confined to a wheelchair, or a less apparent disability like chronic fatigue syndrome.

Having a disability or medical condition in the family does not prevent a person from providing a wonderful environment for a child. We have worked with prospective adoptive families with disabilities who have successfully parented adopted babies. Sometimes they have made adaptations in their home or have had additional assistance with their newborn. As medicine advances, conditions that were once debilitating or even terminal may no longer present such serious threats. Be sure to ask questions and educate yourself before making assumptions in this area.

In an open adoption it is important to discuss with the prospective adoptive family any special circumstance in their home and their plans to make any necessary adjustments to their environment. If you choose a prospective adoptive parent with a disability or medical condition, your counselor can assist you with any questions you may have.

Lesbian, Gay Male, Bisexual and Transgender Parents

Some expectant mothers want to place their child with parents from the LGBT community. Many LGBT couples and singles want to raise children, and many chose adoption as a way to build their families. Birthmothers frequently tell us that they did not choose the family because of their sexual orientation or gender identity, but rather because they had common values or interests. Sometimes birthmothers choose a LGBT family to show their support for LGBT adoptions.

Occasionally a birthmother will tell us she chose a gay male couple to parent her birth child because then she will still be the only mother. While this is technically true, it is important to remember that if you decide to place your child for adoption you will be a birthmother, not a parent. We sometimes find that some birthmothers think they can co-parent in this situation, but adoption, even open adoption, is not co-parenting. Although you will have an important role in your birth child's life, you will not be his or her parent.

Sometimes birthmothers worry about gay men or lesbians parenting a child of the opposite sex, but research and our experience show that this is not a problem. Women raise wonderful boys, and men raise well-adjusted girls. Men and women make equally good parents for boys and girls, and same-sex role models can be grandparents, uncles, aunts, teachers, and friends.

Other birthmothers choose transgender adoptive parents. They most frequently state that gender identity was not the reason for their choice, but rather that they just felt a connection to the family. Other birthmothers told us they chose a family with a transgender person because they wanted to support couples where one or both partners are transgender.[3]

If You Need Financial Help during Your Pregnancy

As we explained in Chapter 1, most states allow prospective adoptive families to pay for pregnancy-related expenses, but what is allowed varies widely from state to state. For example, some states allow prospective adoptive families to only pay for medical expenses, while other states allow payment for all living expenses including rent. In addition, some states have a cap

---

[3] Gender identity (whether you identify as male or female) is separate from sexual orientation. Therefore, families with one or two transgender members can be heterosexual, lesbian, or gay.

on the amount of money that prospective adoptive parents can spend on an expectant mother and may have other restrictions on what expenses they may cover.

If you have financial needs, it is important to discuss them with your adoption counselor. She will work with you to develop a budget. This will also allow her to find families that can meet your financial needs.

In general, we advise an expectant mother to only discuss financial needs with her adoption counselor, as discussion about money with the prospective adoptive family can be very uncomfortable for both parties. Usually the adoptive parents give the money to the adoption agency or attorney who will then pay your expenses directly to the vendor or landlord.

Deciding to Meet the Prospective Adoptive Family

Most expectant mothers meet the prospective adoptive family before making a decision, and are glad they did. There is only so much that an online profile, letter, or even home study can accurately convey. By meeting the prospective family, you can feel much more comfortable with your choice and your vision for the future.

If you are undecided about meeting the family, a good intermediate step is to talk to them on the phone or via video chat. This allows you to get a better idea of who they are without the commitment of meeting. If the call does not go well and you decide they are not the right family for you, you can let your counselor know and spare yourself and the family the emotional investment of a meeting. If everything goes well on the phone or video chat, you will all be more comfortable with each other if you do decide to meet.

Most expectant mothers prefer to narrow their choice to one family to meet and then move on to another family if it does not work out. Other expectant mothers feel the need to meet with two or maybe even three possible adoptive families. While this can be an emotionally draining process, it may be necessary in order to find the family that is right for you.

Meeting the Family

You can meet with the family anywhere that feels comfortable for you—a park, a restaurant, your house, a school, your counselor's office, or maybe the adoption agency office. You may later choose to go to the adoptive family's home, which can give you more information about them. These meetings can last for quite a while, up to several hours, if they are going well.

As nervous as you are to meet the prospective adoptive family, they are likely more nervous than you. The first meeting is really about getting to know each other a little bit and see if there are enough commonalities that you would feel comfortable committing to one another. Agreeing to meet is not a commitment to proceed with an adoption or with that particular family.

Here are some tips for handling the meeting:

- Write your questions down.

- Bring the biological father or a supportive family member or friend.

- Be sure that your adoption counselor has talked to the family ahead of time and set the ground rules (e.g., "Regardless of how our meeting goes, let's all take some time to think about whether we are ready to commit to one another.")

- Bring pictures of family, friends, yourself, and the biological father.

After the meeting call your adoption counselor and tell her your impressions and feelings about the family. Do not hold back if you have any reservations about the family, even if it is just a gut feeling that it is not a good match.

Next you must decide if you want to "match" with this family or continue to look for a more appropriate family. "Matching," means that you want to make a commitment to this family to move ahead and make an adoption plan. A match does not mean you are irrevocably committed to this family; it just means you want to take the next step to find out if this is the right family to parent your child.

The Match Meeting

If you decide you want to match with a particular family, your counselor will set up a "match meeting." At this meeting, you and the adoptive family will share your medical, mental health, social and cultural histories. If your due date is approaching, you will also talk about what you want to happen at the hospital and about contact with the adoptive family after placement (see "The Birth and Hospital Plan" later in this chapter).

Before the match meeting, tell your counselor about any information you want to find out about the adoptive family but may be too shy to bring up yourself. For example, are you concerned that they may have a health problem or about what methods they would use to discipline a child? This will allow the counselor to guide the discussion so as to ensure that you get all the information you need.

In addition, share with the counselor anything you are embarrassed or reluctant to discuss that may be important for the prospective adoptive parents to know. For example, if you drank alcohol during your pregnancy, you should be prepared to explain how much and how frequently you drank. Perhaps you have a mental health condition that runs in your family. This would be important information for the family who parent your child to know so they can provide mental health care if necessary.

Support People

Some expectant mothers find it helpful to have a friend at the meeting for support; sometimes this is the birthfather. If you bring a friend or family member who is supportive of your decision, and whose opinion you value, he or she can help you evaluate your feelings about the meeting afterward.

Other expectant mothers prefer to attend the match meeting alone so their family and friends will not influence their decision. Whether or not you bring a support person with you is entirely your choice. You should do whatever feels most comfortable for you.

Starting the Match Meeting

A match meeting can feel awkward at first. One way to break the ice is to show some pictures of your family and the birthfather (if possible) and ask the family to show you pictures of themselves, family, their home, and fun places they like to go. This allows you to learn a little more about each other in an informal way.

There is a tendency at these first meetings for the focus to be on the expectant mother. It may be more natural for the family to begin asking, "So, when are you due? What does your family think? Do you know if it's a boy or a girl?" and so forth. Of course, you will want to talk to the family about these issues, but you also want to make sure you find out about them.

If the prospective adoptive family is a couple, we start the meeting by talking about how they met each other. All couples like to reminisce about when they first fell in love, and so it is a comfortable (and sometimes funny) way to begin. It is then easier to ask them other questions, like why they want to adopt. With a single prospective adoptive parent we will ask him or her to tell us a little bit about his or her childhood.

You can expect the prospective adoptive family to have a list of questions they want to ask you, too. They probably did not sleep a wink the night before, worrying about what you would think of them. They may have suffered multiple losses—infertility, failed pregnancies, or perhaps a previous adoption attempt that did not work out. In addition, they are probably very excited. They are arriving to meet you with many of the same anxieties, fears, hopes, and dreams as you.

They are also going to be concerned about the risks they may be taking in deciding to work with you. They may be concerned about the birthfather's opinion about the adoption, especially if he is not going to be a part of the adoption planning. They will be worried about the health of the baby. They will wonder if you are serious about your decision. They will want to know everything about you, just as you will want to know everything about them. Although you may not have all of the answers at this time, being forthright with your feelings from the beginning will create a foundation of honesty and trust.

The adoption counselor who facilitates the meeting will be careful to make sure that you and the adoptive family have your questions addressed.

Questions for Prospective Adoptive Families

For All Families:
- Why do you want to adopt?
- How do you plan to tell the child about his/her adoption?
- How do you feel about contact with me? With my extended family? With the biological father?
- What sort of contact do you envision after placement?
- What are your religious beliefs and practices?
- What does your extended family think about adoption?
- How close are you to your extended family? How often do you see them and spend time with them?
- Do you plan to have more children?
- What are your child rearing beliefs and practices?
- Do you have any medical or mental health conditions?
- Are you working with a surrogate, and if that plan works out do you still plan to adopt my baby?

- If my baby has a disability or health problem, would you still want to adopt?
- Under what conditions would you decide not to adopt my baby?

For Two-Parent Families:

- How long have you known each other? How did you meet?
- How long have you been in a relationship?
- Are you married? If so, how long have you been married?

For Single Parent Families:

- Have you ever been married?
- What happens if you meet someone you want to marry? How will you integrate your child into the relationship?

For Heterosexual and Lesbian Families:

- Are you still trying to get pregnant?
- If you become pregnant, would you still want to adopt my baby?

For Families that Already have a Child or Children:

- Have you talked to your other child or children about the adoption? What was the reaction?
- Why do you want another child?
- Tell me how you discipline your child or children.

For Families of a Different Race and/or Ethnicity than You and/or the Biological Father:

- What challenges do you think you will face as a transracial family?

- What have you done to prepare yourselves to become a transracial family?

Questions to Anticipate from the Prospective Adoptive Parents

- When did you first learn you were pregnant?
- How did you come to the decision to place your child for adoption?
- Have you received counseling to help you determine if adoption is the right choice for you?
- Have you received prenatal care? How is your health? How is the baby's health?
- Does the biological father know of your plans? Is he supportive?
- Do you want ongoing contact with us? Do you want visits? Phone calls? Emails?
- How does your family feel about your adoption plans? Do they want to meet us?
- Have you used drugs, alcohol or cigarettes during your pregnancy?
- How sure are you about your adoption decision? What would cause you to change your mind about placing your baby for adoption?

If you find yourself uncomfortable with any of the questions that the adoptive parents ask you, it is your right to ask that the adoption professional facilitate conversations about these topics.

The Birth and Hospital Plan

The birth and hospital plan is a written document explaining what you would like to have happen at the hospital before, during and after giving birth. A birth and hospital plan can serve as a helpful tool to clarify your preferences during your hospital stay. Informing the hospital staff, adoption counselor, and prospective adoptive family of your preferences can make your hospital experience less stressful.

Your adoption professional should have an outline or worksheet for you to complete and can help you with anything you are unsure of. A birth and hospital plan includes who will be with your during the labor and delivery, who will be designated to cut the umbilical cord, who will hold the baby first after delivery, who will spend time with and care for the baby, whether a male baby will be circumcised, and who will make medical decisions for the baby.

Remember to be honest with yourself and true to your feelings. The adoptive parents will participate in the birth and the baby's care to whatever extent you are comfortable. Additionally, you can change the decisions you make about your birth and hospital plan at anytime, even at the last minute. In fact, some agencies use a form called "Tentative Hospital Plan" to emphasize that this plan can change.

This is your plan, and the decisions regarding the birth are up to you. The adoption counselor will facilitate a discussion with you and the prospective adoptive family (sometimes during the match meeting) to ensure that they understand and support your plan. The adoption counselor will send the plan to the hospital and review it with the hospital social worker. If you are planning to use a birthing center or have a home birth, she will provide the plan to the birthing professional with whom you plan to work.

"I really wanted the adoptive parents to be part of the process because I thought it would help the baby to bond with them. I also wanted them to be part of her life from the very beginning. There would not be any part of her life that they did not participate in."

Amanda, 29-year-old birthmother

"I felt really close to the adoptive family of my birth daughter, but I really needed to labor by myself. I needed to get through the pain on my own and I wanted some time where it was

just her and I, so I could say goodbye, before she joined her adoptive family."

Jenny, 41-year-old birthmother

You will also want to talk with the prospective adoptive parents about naming the baby. It is your right to put whatever name you choose on the original birth certificate. There will be a revised birth certificate issued once the court finalizes the adoption that will include the names of the adoptive parent(s) and the name they choose for the baby. Although the adoptive family can choose the name on the revised birth certificates, most prospective adoptive families want to discuss their name choice with you.

In addition, many prospective birthmothers want to discuss the name that the adoptive family is going to give the child. Some prospective adoptive parents and prospective birthmothers discuss first names until they find one they both like. The prospective adoptive parents may ask if the prospective birthmother would choose one of the middle names. If you would like to do this, let your adoption counselor know so she can bring it up during the match meeting. Most prospective adoptive families will honor such a request, and some ask if they can use a prospective birthmother's first name or other special family name as a middle name.

Some birthmothers decide to put a first and middle name of their choice and their last name on the original birth certificate. Many birthmothers feel that giving their child their name on the original birth certificate is a concrete expression of their love and shows that they did not abandon their child. Sometimes both the birthmother and the adoptive family want to give the child the same name on the original and revised birth certificates. Most often, this is a first and middle name both parties agree on, and then the last name or names of the adoptive family.

Naming a child is usually significant for the birth and adoptive families, and it can create a wonderful legacy for the child. There is no right or wrong way to approach naming a child. No matter what you decide, your birth child will know that the naming decision was thoughtful and done out of love.

"The adoptive fathers of my birth son came up with the same name I wanted to name the baby. This made us all laugh and very happy. In addition, they asked if they could use a variation of my first name as his middle name. I felt so honored and delighted by this request."

Janelle, 19-year-old birthmother

"I felt like it was really important that I name my twin birth daughters on their original birth certificates. I felt that naming them showed how much I loved them. As a result, it allowed me to let the adoptive mothers chose whatever names they wanted for the babies on the revised birth certificates without my input."

Patricia, 25-year-old birthmother

Informing the Hospital

Once you have made decisions about your labor and delivery, it is a good idea to let the hospital know about your plans. Your adoption counselor or attorney can send a packet to the hospital social worker and/or head nurse so the hospital is aware of the adoption and your preferences for your birth plan. The packet will probably include releases, allowing the hospital staff to disclose information about the labor and delivery to the prospective adoptive family, as well as to your counselor and attorney (if you wish information to be disclosed). Many times counselors also include information about the prospective adoptive parents, as well as their picture. In case the hospital personnel are unable to locate the paperwork on the day you are admitted, you can ask your adoption counselor to give you and/or the prospective adoptive family an extra copy of the packet to pack in your hospital bag.

If it interests you, you can arrange a tour of the hospital ahead of time. If you would like the adoptive family to attend, this is a great opportunity for everyone to meet the social worker and nursing staff. You can visit the labor, delivery, and postpartum rooms, see the nursery and check out the parking, cafeteria, and waiting rooms.

During the visit, you can ask if the hospital has previously worked with an adoption and find out if there are any restrictions or limitations. Your adoption counselor should also be in contact with the hospital social worker to make sure that all of your preferences in your birth plan fall within the guidelines of the hospital's policies.

Sample Questions for the Hospital Staff

- Have they previously handled open adoptions at their hospital?
- Do they restrict the number of people allowed in the labor and delivery rooms? If so, how many people does the hospital allow?
- Do they have alternative birthing rooms, and if so, are there any requirements for using them?
- Can you have a private room?
- Are there any visiting restrictions for the adoptive family or your family? If so, what are they?
- Do they allow cameras or recording devices in the labor and delivery areas?
- If your baby stays in the nursery, can the adoptive family visit whenever they like? Are there any restrictions?
- What paperwork will you have to sign in order to release your baby to the adoptive family?
- How long can you stay in the hospital if you have no complications?
- What is the hospital discharge policy if the baby is ready to leave the hospital before you are, or vice versa?

Creating a Post-Adoption Contact Agreement

As your due date approaches, the adoption counselor will facilitate a meeting to discuss the post-adoption contact agreement that will outline your wishes and the wishes of the prospective adoptive family for future contact after the placement. These agreements, called "open adoption agreements" or "cooperative adoption agreements" can be a guide in defining your relationship.

Currently, these agreements are legally enforceable in twenty-three states, and we expect more states to follow suit. We encourage you to set up a legally enforceable agreement even if you have a great relationship with the prospective adoptive parents. Asking for a legally enforceable agreement does not mean you don't trust the prospective adoptive family, it just allows you to state exactly what sort of contact you want and to ensure that a court will back your wishes for an open adoption.

Most prospective adoptive families will support your request for an enforceable contact agreement. You should be wary of any prospective adoptive family that tries to talk you out of filing an agreement in court, as it will not be enforceable unless filed with the court when the adoption finalizes.

It is important to determine the laws of the state where you live and the laws in the state where the prospective adoptive family lives. Sometimes, though not always, you can sign the termination of rights paperwork for the state where the potential adoptive family lives, and you may want to do so if that state's laws allow for enforceable contact agreements.

Even if you are unable to have an enforceable contact agreement because neither you nor the adoptive parents live in a state where this is possible, it is important to have some written agreement in place because most adoptive families will honor an agreement they have signed, even if it is not legally enforceable.

One important guideline is to make the agreement as specific as possible so that everyone's expectations are clearly stated. Nevertheless, it can be hard to predict specific requests beyond the child's first birthday. Therefore, it is important to remember that the basis of open adoption is trust, mutual caring and respect between birth and adoptive families. The adoption counselor will encourage everyone to consider the best interests of each other, as well as the child who does not yet have a voice.

The contact agreement should include a discussion about who can post photos of the child on social media and, if so, what restrictions might apply. How often do you want to have photos emailed or mailed? How many visits would you like in the first year and in the years after the first year? Where will these visits happen? How long will the visits last? If travel is required who will pay for it? Do you want the family or adoption provider to let you know when the adoption finalizes?

Other questions to consider are: How many times do you want to talk on the phone, video chat or email each other? Who will initiate contact? How would you prefer the adoptive family to acknowledge Mother's Day or Birthmother's Day (celebrated the Saturday before Mother's Day)? If you have children, would you like them included in the visits? Do you have any other special contact requests?

Although there is no typical agreement, there are general guidelines to consider in developing your contact agreement. First, you may want to think through how much contact you want in the first year after placement. Additionally, you will want to consider how much contact you want until the child is eighteen. Many birthmothers want very regular contact in the first year but some want none. Perhaps you will want to see the baby in her home the first month after placement. Although it may seem counterintuitive, seeing the baby in the adoptive parents' home can be reassuring rather than painful.

You may want to see the family every few months the first year to be assured that everything is going well. After the first year, we encourage families to visit in person a minimum of once a year and to exchange phone calls, video chats, and emails, as well. Although many families visit more frequently, we do not advise including more frequent visitation or contact in the written agreement unless you are sure that more frequent visits are something you will want long-term. This is because it is difficult to predict what will happen during the next 18 years. More frequent visitation might become a burden rather than something everyone looks forward to doing.

Although this can seem like a lot to think about, an agreement can prevent all sorts of misunderstandings down the road. We find that most birth and adoptive families agree that the process of developing the agreement allowed them to set expectations and that after they signed the agreement they rarely looked at it again. They allowed the relationship to develop naturally, and kept to the spirit of the agreement.

Of course, sometimes adoptive families and birthmothers disagree about the contact agreement. If this happens, we encourage you to call your adoption provider, even if it is years later and ask them to help mediate the dispute. Often when there is a misunderstanding that hurt someone's feelings, once everyone has a chance to express all concerns the dispute is usually settled. It is very rare that a birthmother feels she must involve the courts. It is important to understand that the courts in twenty-three states can enforce contact, but they cannot, and will not, overturn the adoption.

"It made me feel really secure in my choice when the adoptive parents suggested I sign termination papers from their state because the contact agreement would be legally enforceable. I knew then that they would never cut me out of their or my birth child's life."

Sofia, 26-year-old birthmother

"I was really worried that the contact agreement was not legally enforceable where I live, but the adoptive parents reassured me that they would always abide by it. It has been five years now, and they are as good as their word."

Gina, 34-year-old birthmother

What if We Live Far Away From Each Other?

When birthmothers choose a prospective adoptive family who lives far away or in another state, an open adoption can still proceed, although both parties have to be creative in addressing the logistical and emotional issues. It is important to have an in-person match meeting. This may require one of you to travel to the other's hometown, but geographic distance should not prevent you from meeting and getting to know one another before the birth.

"We developed a great relationship in the four months before the birth. We talked on the phone and via online video since they lived in Washington. Every month, the adoptive mom would come down and take me to the support group at the adoption agency. We would always have lunch together, and then we might shop for clothes."

Marcella, 20-year-old birthmother

Is This the Right Family for Me?

If you are like most expectant mothers, you will probably have a good idea about how you feel about the prospective adoptive family by the end of the match meeting. Sometimes things just seem to click, and an hour into the meeting, you are talking as if you have known each other for a long time. Other times, you may have an uneasy feeling during the meeting, a gut sense that things just are not right. Talk to your counselor about how you felt about the family, ask yourself the following questions—and then follow your instincts. Do not settle for a situation that just does not seem right.

Questions to Ask Yourself about the Prospective Parents

- Do you feel comfortable with this family?
- Do you want to be in a lifelong relationship with this family?
- Can you trust this family?
- Do you feel this family has respect for you?
- Do you share the same ideas about ongoing contact?
- Can you imagine handing your baby to this family?
- Can you imagine this family being your baby's parent(s)?

What if the Prospective Adoptive Family Decides to Un-Match?

Sometimes the prospective adoptive family will decide that they do not feel comfortable moving forward with the adoption plan and will ask to un-match. There are many reasons that prospective adoptive families decide to un-match; one of the most common is the family's ambivalence about building their family through adoption. While it was not fair for them to match with you before they had worked out their feelings about adoption, it is important to remember that this has nothing do with you.

Another common reason is that the prospective adoptive family found out something about you that makes them uncomfortable. For example, perhaps you revealed you had been using drugs or drinking alcohol during your pregnancy. When a prospective adoptive family wants to un-match it can feel like a personal rejection and even evoke feelings of shame. It is very important to remember that you do not need to judge yourself just because a prospective adoptive family is not comfortable with your situation. There are plenty of families open to adopting your baby who will not judge you. Do not give up if a prospective adoptive family does not want to move forward with you. They just were not the right family for you, so keep looking.

If You Cannot Find a Prospective Adoptive Family for Your Child

When an expectant mother cannot find an appropriate prospective adoptive family for her child, it could mean she is unsure of her decision. She may not be able to imagine anyone being a good enough parent, so she cannot let go and move forward. If you have not yet found parents for your child and you have had the opportunity to select from a fair number of families, it could be time to reevaluate your adoption plan.

Choosing adoption involves a great deal of letting go, not only of the child, but also of the ideal of "perfect parenting." After taking the responsibility of finding a family for the child, expectant mothers should be able to say, "I've done the best I can with the best intentions." If you find that you cannot do that, adoption may not be the right choice for you.

Understanding the Viewpoint of the Prospective Adoptive Parents

As with expectant mothers, no two prospective adoptive families are alike. There are, however, common experiences prospective adoptive parents may share that will influence the way they approach adoption. A common, though not universal, experience for many heterosexual and lesbian adoptive parents is a struggle with infertility. Gay men who are coming out often struggle with the fact that they may never become a biological parent; sometimes they also struggle with infertility issues when they explore options for building their family. Sometimes this is the first time they have really acknowledged the difficulties they face in building a biological family, or perhaps they have had a surrogate miscarry or fail to become pregnant.

Infertility can exact a high emotional and financial toll. Often, by the time a family struggling with infertility contacts an adoption organization, they have spent a number of years trying to have a baby. This process can be extremely upsetting especially if the family has made repeated unsuccessful attempts to have a biological child.

"We feel so damaged. We always wanted children, and it feels like we are such failures that we cannot have one biologically."

Jenna and Gary, 43-year-old and 42-year-old prospective adoptive parents

The losses families endure through infertility can affect their readiness to adopt and the relationship they build with their child's birth family. Agencies will help prospective adoptive families explore their infertility, their losses, how they view adoption after their infertility experience, and how they feel about moving on. In some cases, agencies may recommend further counseling for the family to help heal the wounds from their infertility experience and prepare them more fully for their adoption journey.

In the past, open adoption experts thought it mattered little whether or not the adopting family had resolved their grief about their inability to have biological children. Expectant mothers would place their children for adoption and were never seen or heard from again. With open adoption, expectant mothers and the prospective adoptive family meet, and most open adoptions involve a lifetime relationship. This openness means the adoptive families must deal on a regular basis with the fact that they are not the biological parents of the child.

For some prospective adoptive families openness can initially be very confusing and threatening. How can they truly feel like parents when there is another parent they must meet and get to know? Will the expectant mother ever go away and let them become the parents they have always wanted to be? Unless the prospective adoptive family has had some personal experience with adoption, has done a lot of reading, or has asked many questions, they may be uneasy with the idea of openness.

Many of the conflicts that may surface during the course of your relationship with the family have their roots in fear. Your fear is that the family will not love your child or will not honor their word to allow you to be part of their lives after the adoption finalizes. Their fear is that you will not be able to let go of the baby and let them parent.

A skilled counselor can help facilitate the good communication needed to address these fears, especially if you do not know each other well. Each of you is treading lightly with the other, hoping not to offend or say the wrong thing. A counselor who is experienced in adoption can make a tremendous difference as you navigate the early days of your relationship.

CHAPTER 4: MOVING AHEAD WITH YOUR ADOPTION PLAN

While some birthparents begin to make their adoption plan in the first trimester, others wait until later in the pregnancy, until the birth, or even until they have tried parenting for a while. There is no right or wrong time to decide on adoption, but there are some typical processes to go through mentally, emotionally, and legally.

One important step in preparing for an adoption is to continue building a relationship with the prospective adoptive family. Naturally, this relationship can take many forms, depending on the kind of openness you desire. Assuming that you have selected a prospective adoptive family for your child, you can move on to the next step, which is building a strong relationship through regular contact and good communication.

The "Honeymoon Period"

Many birthparents speak of an initial "honeymoon period" with the prospective adoptive family they have chosen. If you live close enough, you may wish to spend time with them throughout your pregnancy. It is also possible that you will prefer less contact; it all depends on your comfort level.

You might want to get together informally for a meal, an outing, or to see their home and neighborhood. Even if they live far away, some birthmothers choose to travel to the prospective adoptive family's community to see the neighborhood where the child will grow up, the school he or she will attend, or the park where he or she will play.

There also may be people in the prospective adoptive family's life that they would like you to meet. It may be more reassuring when the time comes to say good-bye to your child if you already have a picture in your mind's eye of the house where the child will be living and the people who will love him or her. If the logistics of your life make it too difficult for you to travel, the prospective adoptive parents can travel to you for a visit. There may be people in your life—friends, family, and children, for example—whom you would like the prospective adoptive family to meet.

Where the adoption counselor works might also be a factor in determining who visits whom for the match meeting. Having your counselor available to facilitate the meeting in person can be extremely helpful in the beginning stages of building your relationship.

Sometimes the prospective adoptive family wants to accompany you to a prenatal medical appointment. For most prospective adoptive families, this is their way of connecting to you and your baby. Hearing the baby's heartbeat or actually viewing the baby during an ultrasound may be the closest an adoptive family will come to participating in a pregnancy. This arrangement is your decision, however, and must be something with which you are comfortable. This is your pregnancy, your body, and your baby until you say differently. It is up to you to decide how much of your pregnancy you want to share with others.

At this stage of your relationship with the prospective adoptive family, you may be wavering about the degree of closeness you want now and in the future with the prospective adoptive family and, eventually, with the child. On the one hand, closeness enables you to feel connected. On the other hand, too much contact may feel invasive or burdensome. Although you do not have to decide this today, you may wish to give some thought as to what feels most appropriate to you. It is important to be able to set privacy boundaries if you feel the need.

"During my pregnancy, the adoptive mom and I got really close. We had a lot in common. The adoptive father felt like a big brother. I felt like they were part of my family."

Peggy, 23-year-old birthmother

"The adoptive moms and I texted a couple of times a week, and we went to lunch a few times, but I felt kind of funny getting too close to them, so I decided to keep my distance. Actually, the father of the child was really the one who kept in touch with them."

Kaitlyn, 30-year-old birthmother

"My relationship with the adoptive family before the birth wasn't as close as it became after the birth. Before the birth, we only got together twice: once for our match meeting, and once for a barbecue at my parents' home."

Maria, 17-year-old birthmother

If you and the prospective adoptive family are getting along well, you may be tempted to talk less regularly with your counselor, or you may feel that counseling is now less important. It is common to think that counseling is not needed when things are going well, but try to keep in mind that you may feel a wide range of emotions during your pregnancy and the adoptive placement. If you are not building a relationship with your adoption counselor now, it will feel awkward to reach out to her when your feelings become stronger or more painful.

Handling Disagreements

In open adoption, everyone is choosing to take on additional relatives, and even in the best of circumstances relatives will have moments of disagreement or misunderstanding. It is completely normal to experience conflict while you are building your relationship, and it can even have a positive impact in the end. If you can get through a disagreement during the pregnancy, it will help prepare you for resolving future conflicts after the baby arrives and the emotional temperature escalates.

It is very important that you are able to talk with the prospective adoptive family about things that really matter to you. If you find yourself biting your tongue for fear of saying something that may upset them, or if you feel you are avoiding a topic you know is important to discuss, ask your counselor for help. The prospective adoptive family should also have a counselor they can consult about their challenging feelings. If something is really bothering you about how things are progressing, discuss your feelings with your counselor. The problem will not often go away by itself, and you may need some discussion to clear the air.

At some point, you may even feel resentful or jealous as you get in touch with the reality of losing your role as the mother. Although you are having conflicted feelings toward the adoptive parents, your relationship with them is at a delicate stage. It is important to use your counselor as a facilitator instead of directing the negativity towards the adoptive parents.

One of the most toxic phases of any match is the "walking on eggshells" syndrome, when the birthparent and/or the prospective adoptive family are struggling with strong negative feelings. Maybe you or the prospective adoptive parent or parents come from a family where the direct and honest expression of feelings is not the norm. With the help of the adoption counselor you and/or the adoptive family can learn to communicate emotions appropriately. This is important for the development of a healthy adoption.

It is normal for the level of comfort you feel with the prospective adoptive family to ebb and flow. Give yourself a lot of latitude through this adoption process. It is hard to predict exactly how you will feel, and having some compassion for yourself will help.

Sensitivity to the Prospective Adoptive Family

The ability to empathize with the prospective adoptive family will be very helpful. Chances are that this is their first time going through an adoption, and they will be as anxious and unsure of the process as you are.

The media has run many stories about "adoptions gone bad" that can scare prospective adoptive families. These include television shows featuring sensational stories about birthparents who take their baby back or embezzle tens of thousands of dollars from unsuspecting prospective adoptive families. The prospective adoptive family's friends and relatives may be questioning their decision to participate in an open adoption and may need education about its benefits. It is often necessary to provide people with additional information to counteract the stereotype of the "unstable birthmother" that has been portrayed in popular entertainment.

As we have previously discussed, many people who choose to create their family through adoption have suffered infertility problems. This often involves years of invasive, unsuccessful, and financially draining procedures that strip people of their sense of control and leave emotional wounds. The potential adoptive family may be wondering if they are equipped to be good parents.

Your sensitivity to issues like these will help the prospective adoptive family feel they "deserve" to be your child's parents. Communicating your understanding of their feelings will go a long way toward establishing mutual respect and consideration. Reassuring the adoptive family of your confidence in them may help with their fears about the process.

"We waited so long and went through so much to adopt a baby, but when we were finally blessed with a child, I felt like a fraud. I felt like I was pretending to be a real parent, when I knew I was not. I felt the need to cover up the fact that this child was not biologically ours. I also felt a great burden on my shoulders—I had to be the perfect parent. After all, someone entrusted me with a child who was a miracle in my eyes; I had to be the perfect mother in return. It took me months to realize that becoming an adoptive

mother was becoming a real parent, and that my child's differences from us were what made her so beautiful. I also finally realized that nobody is a perfect parent. We all just have the responsibility to try our hardest and be the best role models for our children. Looking back on this now, I wish our child's birthmother had verbally given us her permission during the adoption process to parent her child. I wish she had said that she didn't expect perfection from us, just our very best."

Stephanie, 37-year-old adoptive mother

Over the course of the match, it will be very helpful if you and the adoptive family can develop tolerance and acceptance for one another. Each of you will have idiosyncrasies that may seem foreign to the other. Acceptance of differences can be a healthy part of any long-term relationship.

Some birthmothers report feeling "placement void" if communication with the adoptive family decreases after the placement. Not only are they feeling the loss of their baby, but they are also experiencing a loss due to the change in the relationship with the adoptive family. It can feel bittersweet to see the adoptive family focusing so much on the new baby when they previously focused all their attention on you. Although you will intellectually understand this shift, it can still take an emotional toll.

Living with the Potential Adoptive Family

Sometimes an expectant mother moves to a residence close to the prospective adoptive family during the last part of her pregnancy. On rare occasions, a birthmother might stay with the prospective adoptive family for the last few weeks before the birth.

There are pros and cons to an arrangement like this. On the positive side, it will allow you to get to know the family intimately. You can all prepare for the birth of the baby together, and, if all goes well, you will feel supported, loved, and nurtured by the family to whom you are entrusting your baby. However, this type of arrangement requires that people be quite flexible, as well as good communicators.

This kind of closeness will most likely bring up conflict, and the prospective birthmother and the prospective adoptive family will have to be committed to working through the difficulties that will naturally arise. Additionally, this arrangement would mean leaving your family and friends. Even if you spend a good amount of time with the adoptive family, you might feel isolated and lonely. Birthmothers have also reported that saying good-bye after the baby is born is especially difficult if it also means moving out of the adoptive family's home.

Many adoption professionals caution against this type of arrangement for another reason. They feel that by living with the prospective adoptive family during your pregnancy, your sense of obligation to them will increase. This could make it difficult for you to choose to parent the baby because you might feel hesitant to do so after all they have done for you.

A Few Words about Counseling

Expectant mothers come into the adoption process with varied opinions about counseling. Some have had very positive relationships with counselors; others have found counseling unhelpful or even harmful. Regardless of your previous experience, most adoption professionals strongly recommend that you have some kind of professional guidance. There are many challenges as you navigate the uncertainty of adoption, and having a supportive advocate can be essential.

"I wish I had received more counseling when it was new and raw because I am so distanced now—I think I just stuffed my feelings."

Olivia, 25-year-old birthmother

How an Adoption Counselor Can Help You

An adoption counselor can provide you with logistical and emotional information to prepare you for what is to come. She can advocate for you to ensure that you are creating the kind of adoption that you envision. She can listen to your thoughts and feelings and provide support. For all of these reasons and more, it is especially important for you to feel comfortable with your counselor. Make sure it is a good fit.

Let your counselor know what you expect from counseling. Some expectant mothers want a counselor to guide them in making decisions, others simply want emotional support for the decisions they have already made, and still others only need help moving from step to step.

Some agencies have separate counselors for the prospective birthmother and the prospective adoptive family, but most agencies have the same counselor work with the prospective birthmother and the prospective adoptive family. If your counselor is also working with the prospective adoptive family, make sure you ask your counselor what information she will share with the prospective adoptive family and what will be confidential.

This would also be a good time to attend a birthparent support group, if there are any in your area, or to get the phone numbers or email addresses of other birthmothers you can call for support. Your adoption professional may be able to match you up with an alumna birthmother to talk with or they might have an online support network where you can connect with other birthmothers.

You can also contact Birthmom Buds at www.birthmombuds.com. This is an organization founded and run by birthmothers that can help you find other birthmothers willing to provide support. Hearing from other birthmothers will reassure you that what you are experiencing is normal. Additionally, being able to talk to those that have "been there" can help to minimize any sense of isolation you may be feeling.

CHAPTER 5: YOUR PREGNANCY

"I felt overwhelmed and lonely."

Zoe, 22-year-old birthmother

"Depressed, stressed, in denial, scared, and betrayed, but also happy in a way."

Diana, 16-year-old birthmother

"Excited!"

Mona, 31-year-old birthmother

"I hardly had time to experience my pregnancy. I felt like my life was so screwed up."

Roberta, 24-year-old birthmother

"I was in shock. I felt very upset and worried because I didn't find out that I was pregnant until I was about eight months along. I was going through mass confusion and trying to figure out how to break the news to everyone and handle the rejection I would get in return."

Ellie, 21-year-old birthmother

The above are all feelings women have expressed to us upon learning of their unplanned pregnancy. Although many women acknowledge their pregnancies very early on and begin to think about their options, other women experience denial or detachment for many months. Some fear that if they admit they are pregnant, they will then have to do something about it. Others are trying to protect themselves from the emotional pain they feel is inevitable. As you eventually allow yourself to face your predicament, there will come a point when you have to make some decisions about your pregnancy.

Your Pregnancy

Once you find out you are pregnant, you have many decisions to make. Take it slowly. There is no need at this point to rush into a decision, no matter how far along you are. Take time to absorb the fact and experience all the emotions that will most likely occur, such as shock, fear, happiness, anger, or relief.

As your pregnancy progresses the physical signs and symptoms will become apparent. You may feel slow, sluggish, tired, or grumpy. You may find the ways in which your body is changing to be distressing, or worry how your pregnancy might affect your romantic relationships. You may be very scared that people in your life will figure it out before you feel ready to tell them. At other times, you may love being pregnant.

"I had a great pregnancy. I was so excited about the baby and the whole idea of being pregnant. I enjoyed the ultrasound and found out it was going to be a boy. One of the neatest parts was

lying in bed at night and watching him move around in my
stomach. It was a very positive experience. "

Karen, 37-year-old birthmother

You may find you are getting lots of attention and people
around you are kinder and more considerate. People in public may
smile and wish you well. How you choose to respond to this
attention is entirely up to you. Even well intentioned questions can
be very uncomfortable for women considering adoption.

Do not feel obligated to tell strangers the details of your
situation. You have a right to maintain your privacy about your
decision to place. While some expectant women see themselves as
ambassadors of adoption and enjoy educating people, others feel
more comfortable graciously exiting the conversation.

Your pregnancy will undoubtedly bring about a multitude
of feelings for you, ranging from joy to despair. For a woman
making an adoption plan all of these emotions are to be expected.

Fear and Expectations

"If I love my baby now, will I ever be able to let her go?"

Lottie, 34-year-old birthmother

If you have decided on adoption, you will ask yourself this
question many times during your pregnancy. You may try to
remain detached as you go through your pregnancy because you
think it will be easier to place your baby with the adoptive family
when the time comes. However, as much as you want to stay
detached, you will bond with your baby. Maybe it is not a
conscious attachment, but you may wake up one day with an
overpowering love for the baby you are carrying. This may happen
the first time you feel your baby kick or when you see your first
ultrasound.

Even if you never thought you wanted to be a mom, it is difficult not to feel love for your baby. Bonding with your baby does not mean you cannot place him or her for adoption, nor does it prevent the adoptive family from bonding with the baby after the birth and placement.

You may be afraid to show how excited or content you are in front of the prospective adoptive family, your parents, or your partner because you are worried they might think you are changing your mind about the adoption. Allowing yourself to feel happy, sad, fearful or content does not need to disrupt your adoption plan. These feelings are part of the normal range of emotions for all pregnant women, and to some extent you will feel these things whether you parent your baby or place him or her for adoption.

"I pretty much ignored the pregnancy. I didn't realize it would be the only one I would ever have, so I stayed away from learning anything about it. I just let it happen. I always loved the baby, but I knew I would place her for adoption. But I loved playing with her while I carried her."

Ana, 27-year-old birthmother

"It's a Girl!"

You may have decided to place your baby for adoption before finding out its sex. An ultrasound test can usually tell the sex of the baby, and most women today have an ultrasound sometime during their pregnancy. You may also have genetic testing or an amniocentesis, if your doctor recommends it, which will identify the baby's sex.

Discovering your baby's sex can alter your feelings about the placement momentarily or permanently. If you have only sons, you may not be able to imagine giving up the chance to raise a daughter. Alternatively, maybe you believe boys are easier to parent then girls. Perhaps when the birthfather learns he is the father of a son the baby will suddenly become a reality to him, and he will not agree with adoption anymore.

Finding out the baby's sex can make the child more real. Take time to explore your feelings about parenting or placing a baby boy or baby girl to see if the sex of the baby will affect your decision.

Twins (or More)

Finding out you are pregnant with twins may complicate your adoption decision. Although caring for twins is more difficult than caring for one baby, there can be an emotional pull toward parenting twins. Many cities have resources for the parents of twins, and you can ask your medical practitioner or counselor for a referral to these organizations. They might be able to put you in touch with other parents of twins you can talk to about the reality of having two babies.

If you are pregnant with multiple babies, it is important to know that there is substantial research showing it is best to have twins or triplets raised in the same family. It may be tempting to decide you want to parent one and place the other or perhaps to place with two different families, but this is not in the best interest of the children. Most agencies and adoption attorneys will not agree to separate twins or triplets in adoptive placements.

Traumatic Situations and Their Effect on Adoption Placement

Some women become pregnant as the result of incest or rape. Other women are pregnant by abusive partners. In addition to dealing with an unwanted pregnancy, these women are also dealing with overwhelming feelings of rage, resentment, fear, and guilt. If you are in this situation, it is essential that you seek help from professionals who are expert in dealing with violence against women. Call the National Domestic Violence Hotline at 800-799-7233 or go to the following website: www.thehotline.org/help/.

You may decide to carry the pregnancy to term but still have mixed feelings about the pregnancy and the baby. Some of your anger toward the perpetrator may get confused with your feelings for your baby, even though you can intellectually distinguish between the person who caused you harm and your unborn child. Alternatively, you may realize after the birth that these issues do not actually impede your ability to love your child.

Remember that you are dealing with two crises at once, which is an overload for anyone. It is sometimes hard to ask for and receive the support you need. However, it is imperative to muster as much support for yourself as possible. Seek out people who are non-judgmental and caring. You may want help to talk with the prospective adoptive family about the circumstances surrounding your pregnancy, and this is a very important time to have a counselor or support person available.

Preparing for the Delivery

"Before the birth, I felt guilty because I couldn't give my little girl the things she needed to be healthy and happy once she was born. It was difficult preparing myself for the birth and eventual relinquishment of my rights. I loved my baby from the time I learned I was pregnant. It was because I loved her so much that I was able to consider adoption in the first place."

Robin, 30-year-old birthmother

As your pregnancy progresses, you will start thinking about childbirth. If this is your first pregnancy, the unknown aspects of giving birth can be scary. You may develop fears and apprehensions about delivering a baby, especially when you begin to hear other women's horror stories of labor and delivery. The following are some choices you can make during this time to help alleviate some of your fears.

Childbirth Preparation Classes

You may want to learn as much as possible about the birthing process so you will be prepared to participate in your labor and delivery to the fullest extent possible. Most hospitals offer childbirth preparation classes or can give you information about where you can find a class. You may also want to ask your adoption counselor if he or she can recommend a private childbirth educator or a video on childbirth.

Childbirth education classes can be an excellent way to prepare yourself for your delivery, but they are generally full of excited families anticipating parenting, and this type of setting may feel uncomfortable. Some people have attended the classes with their support person, and/or the prospective adoptive parent or parents and found them to be welcoming and inclusive. Talking to the person leading the class before you attend is the best way to gauge if it will be a welcoming environment.

A private childbirth educator can offer information and support in a more intimate setting, and you can invite whomever you want to attend. Before inviting the prospective adoptive family, you want to decide whether you actually want them to be present for the delivery. Most prospective adoptive parents are delighted to be involved but also understand if you are not comfortable having them in the room during the birth.

This is also the time to begin thinking about who will be your coach during labor. This might be your partner (whether or not he is the biological father of the child), a friend, relative, or the prospective adoptive parent or parents. Having a support person who can totally focus on you and your needs during your labor can be invaluable.

Prenatal Visits

If you have chosen the prospective adoptive parent or parents before your delivery, you may want to involve them in your prenatal care. Some expectant mothers are comfortable with this and enjoy having the prospective adoptive family accompany them to their doctor appointments, while others feel it is a private and personal experience. Either way is fine, but it needs to be your choice.

Prospective adoptive families are often anxious about your prenatal care and the health of the baby, but it is not appropriate for them to accompany you to your doctor visits without being invited or to contact your doctor without your permission.

Medical Insurance and Other Pregnancy-Related Expenses

Many women delay seeking medical care until late in their pregnancies because they do not have medical insurance. If you do not have insurance of your own or through your parents, you are most likely eligible for Medicaid in the state where you live.

In addition, you may be able to obtain insurance through the Affordable Care Act. Even if the annual enrollment period has ended, a pregnancy is a life change that allows you to participate in the Special Enrollment Period of the Affordable Care Act. You can find answers to all your questions about health insurance at www.healthcare.gov .

If you have insurance through your work, check your company's current health plan. If you have insurance through your parents' plan but do not want them to know yet about your pregnancy, check with an insurance company representative to find out if your parents will receive any correspondence related to your pregnancy care.

Another option for medical coverage is to ask the prospective adoptive family to assist with medical expenses. Check with your attorney or an adoption agency to see if this is legal in your state.

There are additional issues to consider if you are asking the prospective adoptive family to help with medical or other pregnancy-related expenses. For example, will you feel more obligated to place your baby with the prospective adoptive family if they are paying your bills, even though you may want to change your mind?

If you and the prospective adoptive family agree on an arrangement for financial assistance, make sure you are both clear about the expectations and involvement during your pregnancy. You may decide how involved you want the prospective adoptive parents to be in your prenatal care. Are you comfortable with the prospective adoptive parents calling your doctor for updates on your health care or would you prefer that your adoption professional handle any interactions with your physician? Do you want the prospective adoptive parents to join you for the prenatal visits? It is important to be honest about your feelings.

If you do need assistance while you are pregnant, your adoption professional can explain to you the state-specific rules that will apply in your case. Your counselor will also help you create an agreement that both parties feel comfortable with. There should be very clear expectations about how and when you will receive the assistance. Many times the adoption professional acts as an intermediary to keep track of all expenses paid. Assistance is often in the form of a gift card or payment may be sent directly to the vendor, such as a landlord or utility company.

In most states, pregnancy-related expenses are a gift from the potential adoptive family, and there is no obligation on your part to repay these expenses if you decide to parent. However, if the prospective adoptive family pays for this expense and then you decide to parent, the financial loss to them could be quite exorbitant. Additionally, you may feel terribly guilty about changing your mind and causing them financial hardship.

Your counselor or attorney can help you and the prospective adoptive family to work out a clear agreement about pregnancy-related expenses and mediate if there are misunderstandings. Be sure to have someone available to help with this before you accept any money for medical care. In some states you may need permission from the court or may have to fill out financial request forms before receiving assistance.

Some of the best hospitals and medical practitioners we work with accept government-funded health insurance (Medicaid). Many of these doctors and hospitals offer support and guidance to women choosing adoption during the pregnancy and the postpartum period. The doctors, nurses, midwives, and social workers in hospitals are usually supportive of adoption and are willing to work with expectant mothers and prospective adoptive families to implement their wishes.

Of course, there are exceptions. Sometimes health care workers are unsupportive or judgmental. This is unprofessional behavior and has nothing to do with your adoption decision. If a health care worker says something that offends, ask for someone else to work with you.

If you do not know where to start looking for health care, here are some tips:

- Look on the Internet for the local health clinic or public hospital. Ask if you need to have insurance before a prenatal visit. Many public hospitals have financial offices where you can fill out your eligibility paperwork and social workers that can help you walk through the process.
- If you have private insurance but do not have an OB/GYN, ask for a list of doctors who will take patients with your health plan. Private health plans have the names of doctors who accept new patients, often based on due dates. The later in your pregnancy, the more limited your choice of a health care practitioner may be.
- Many large Health Maintenance Organizations (HMOs) will set up your first prenatal visit if you call your local hospital or clinic. You may need to be a member, although some HMOs accept Medicaid as payment. They will assign you a doctor or nurse practitioner.
- Ask friends, relatives, or co-workers if they can recommend a doctor who accepts the type of insurance you have.
- If you have selected a prospective adoptive family, ask them to help you find a doctor or midwife. Most prospective adoptive families are happy to assist.
- Ask your counselor, your adoption social worker, or your attorney for referrals or assistance in finding good, supportive, high-quality medical care. They probably have some very good information and personal knowledge about

doctors, insurance, and how to find the very best medical care available.

Drugs, Alcohol, and Cigarettes

As difficult as it may be, if you have used drugs, alcohol, or cigarettes during your pregnancy, it is very important to talk with your health care practitioner about it. This is a health issue, and your doctor will make appropriate treatment recommendations. Not only is it important to consult with your adoption counselor about informing the prospective adoptive family of your baby's exposure to alcohol or drugs, but you may also need your counselor's help in alerting the hospital so the staff may adequately prepare.

Almost all hospitals test newborns and mothers for drug and alcohol exposure. If your baby tests positive for drugs at the hospital, the hospital staff may be obligated to report this to child welfare. Some states require child welfare to approve a voluntary adoption of your choosing. Regardless, most child welfare workers will allow the placement to move forward even if they are not required to do so by law, especially if the adoption plan was in place before the birth. If your adoption social worker and prospective adoptive family know about any possible drug or alcohol exposure ahead of time, they can more effectively advocate for your adoption plan.

Breastfeeding

Although it is uncommon, some birthmothers do breastfeed even though they have an adoption plan. You may fear that if you breastfeed, you will not be able to part with your baby when it is time to place him for adoption. Although many birthmothers report that breastfeeding does increase the feelings of bonding, you should make the decision based on what feels right to you and not on the judgments of others.

Birthmothers who breastfeed do so for a number of reasons: to have a period of closeness with the baby, for the health and nutritional advantage, or because it is a special experience. If you are considering breastfeeding, it is helpful to discuss it beforehand with the prospective adoptive family, adoption social worker, and your health care practitioner. That way, everyone's expectations will be clear, and there will not be any negative reactions or pressure after the birth.

Many hospitals insist that all women who give birth meet with a lactation specialist who encourages breastfeeding. This may not be appropriate when there is an adoption plan, so make sure the hospital knows you have one.

If you would prefer not to breastfeed but want your child to receive the benefits of the colostrum that your body creates during the late stages of your pregnancy, the hospital can arrange a breast pump for you to use while you are in the hospital.

Some birthmothers have wanted to continue to provide their breast milk after hospital discharge. This is something that needs to feel comfortable to both you and the adoptive family. If you live close to each other, you or the adoptive family can make arrangements for the breast milk to be picked up from your home and delivered to the adoptive parents every few days.

If you live far away from each other but still want to arrange this, there are specialty delivery services that cater to these situations. Before deciding to continue pumping after discharge, talk to your doctor about the possible hormonal consequences. Depending on your sensitivity to hormone changes, continuing to pump may make it more difficult to stabilize your emotions during the healing process after placement.

Some adoptive mothers are also interested in breastfeeding. This is possible with advance planning and often requires the adoptive mother to take hormones to stimulate milk production, but it can be a pleasant transition for your baby.

"I wanted my baby to have the extra nutrition that breast milk provided. I pumped milk in the hospital and continued to pump milk for a few months after the delivery. Twice a week, I

would bring it to the adoptive family or they would pick it up from me."

Rachel, 19-year-old birthmother

"I didn't want to breastfeed, but I liked that the adoptive mother wanted to try breastfeeding. I could see that it helped her bonding with the baby."

Deidre, 16-year-old birthmother

Although there is a lot of publicity about the benefits of breastfeeding, there is substantial evidence showing that children who are not breastfed also grow up healthy. In other words, you can choose whatever feels best for you without any guilt.

"Breastfeeding was not an option for me or the gay male adoptive family I chose. Two years later my birth son is as healthy as could be."

Shelia, 39-year-old birthmother

Alternative Birth Locations

You may decide you want to deliver at home, use a midwife instead of a doctor, or deliver in an alternative birthing center instead of a conventional delivery room. This is an important conversation to have with the adoptive family, as well. If it is something central to your birth plan and the adoptive family is not open to it, you may need to talk to your adoption counselor about whether or not this is the right match for you.

If you are interested in exploring alternative birthing options and plans, there are many books and websites with information about your options. Your doctor and local pregnancy clinic may have some names of midwives that assist in home births or hospital deliveries. In some states, however, midwives are illegal. In addition, certain insurance companies will not pay for a home delivery or a midwife even in states where they are legal so make sure to know all of your resources before making a definite plan.

Family, Friends, and You

"My family was very supportive, and I could always talk to them about anything. My boyfriend was a wonderful support and was behind me every step of the way."

Dahlia, 18-year-old birthmother

"They respected my decision, but I think they thought I would never go through with it. My father still hasn't forgiven my boyfriend or my mother for not trying to talk me out of it."

Ariel, 25-year-old birthmother

"My mother was always there for me when I needed to talk or a shoulder to cry on. I wouldn't have made it without her."

Rosie, 23-year-old birthmother

Almost everyone in your life who knows about your pregnancy and adoption plan will have a reaction, an opinion, or advice. Some of this may be helpful and some distressing. You should think about soliciting help only from those people who will offer you unconditional support.

The quality of the relationship with your family members will probably have a lot to do with whether or not you confide in them. Many times parents will react with disbelief, then anger, followed by understanding and support when the shock wears off. Some family members may never support your decision and may, in fact, make the pregnancy and adoption process even more difficult by sabotaging your efforts.

Your decision to place your child for adoption is a personal and confidential matter and in most states you will not need your parents' permission to proceed. Consult with an attorney or your adoption counselor if you have any questions about laws pertaining to parental involvement. If you cannot talk to your parents, try confiding in a sibling or close relative first. Again, try to choose someone who will support your decision, whether or not they would make the same decision if they were in your shoes.

"Whenever my dad sees me sad, he tells me to cheer up because I did the right thing."

Alexandria, 22-year-old birthmother

"My sister keeps telling me not to be so depressed. She says I should be grateful because I'll still be able to see him as he grows up."

Mollie, 17-year-old birthmother

"I don't understand how my mom isn't sad about this too. It may be my baby but it's her grandchild and I seem to be the only one grieving."

Lauren, 26-year-old birthmother

Reactions like these can feel offensive, as if your family members are invalidating your loss. In reality, people who care about you are saying what they think might make you feel better. Moreover, even though your parents might not be transparent in their grief, they are most likely going through a very difficult emotional process as well. Parents innately want to protect their children, and they might believe that they need to handle their emotions privately in order be strong for you. Accordingly, you may need to communicate to your loved ones what you need from them to feel comforted. That could mean asking them to share their sadness with you so you feel less alone.

Your friends can be the most important source of comfort and support, especially if your family or the birthfather is uninvolved or unsupportive. Having a good friend to talk to, someone with whom to laugh and cry, may be the most valuable support you receive. Be willing to also tell your friends what you need, and they will most likely be there to offer a shoulder or a hug.

Talking With Your Other Children About Your Pregnancy and Adoption Plan

"I think it has been really helpful that my kids are part of the open adoption. They see Sam every year during our visit with the adoptive family. We talk about the adoption, but the most important thing is that they are able to have a relationship with their birth brother."

Adrienne, 25-year-old birthmother

"My daughter was really afraid after the adoption, but once I reassured her that she was staying with me, and that we would see her birth sister again, she felt better."

Sandy, 20-year-old birthmother

Many expectant parents who have children struggle with how and when to tell them about the pregnancy and adoption plan. Some of the most frequent questions we get from prospective birthparents involve talking to their children. Most children, even very young ones, can sense that "something's up." One young mother, who had not yet discussed her pregnancy with her children, recalls admonishing her son and saying he was a nuisance. He replied, "Mothers who don't tell their children that they're pregnant are a nuisance!"

Kids react differently, depending on their age, developmental stage, and temperament. Young children need a lot of reassurance and concrete explanations. They are often worried about themselves and their place in your family and may fear that if you place this baby for adoption, you might place them for adoption, too. Use clear language, and do not be afraid to use the word adoption so that it will be a normal part of your young child's vocabulary. Saying things like, "Baby Justin went away" or "Suzanne isn't going to live with us right now" will only confuse your child, who may wonder where Baby Justin went or when Suzanne will live with you again.

It is important to stress the fact that, "although Baby Heather will live with Bill and Cindy, you will always live with me." Young children can be very literal so it is important to explain that just because Baby Heather will live with another family, they will always live with you and this will never change. Storybooks about adoption with pictures can be a big help. (There are suggested books for children at the end of this book.)

Younger children often benefit from seeing the adoptive family's home so they have a picture in their mind's eye about where the baby will live. Picturing the baby in his or her room is reassuring and helps dispel the fantasy that the baby has just disappeared into thin air. Spending time with them will allow your children to feel more comfortable and confident about the adoption.

"My husband and I have a four-year-old son but we can't take on another child. We talked with our son about how lucky we are to be his Mommy and Daddy, and that he will be with us forever. He has come to adore Jessica and Jason, and we explained that Jessica's tummy is broken so they cannot have a baby on their own. We talked about how the baby I am growing will be their baby so they can also be a Mommy and Daddy. Later

that day, my son told my mom that our family was going to help Jessica and Jason become a family too."

Joanna, 22-year-old birthmother

"I had a three-year-old daughter at the time of the placement. She met the prospective adoptive family. She asks about her birth sister, and we look at pictures together. Every once in a while she tells me that she wants her sister to come home. I explain that she lives with her parents now and not in Mommy's tummy anymore. The pictures help a lot, though, and the fact that she knows where her birth sister lives, and that we get to visit every year."

Savannah, 19-year-old birthmother

Older children may want to be involved in the process and may ask if they can still visit their birth brother or sister. Including your kids in the relationship with the prospective adoptive family may ease some of your children's fears. We have included school-aged children in some of our counseling sessions, especially when discussing ongoing contact.

Some of these kids decide on their own that they would like to send cards or pictures to their birth sibling. Discuss your child's concerns and wishes with the prospective adoptive family before the birth, if possible, so that you can agree on an acceptable level of contact between them and your children. It is important to work with a prospective adoptive family that believes contact between siblings is a healthy part of an open adoption.

If the prospective adoptive family has other children, biological or adopted, they may wonder about the effect of ongoing contact on their other children. Some families struggle with openness when they have more than one adopted child and one child's birth family is more involved than the other child's birth family. If you are going to have a greater level of involvement than another birthparent, discuss with the adoptive family how this will affect all of the children involved. Most birthparents we work with generously interact with the child whose birthparents do not call or visit.

Even though you placed your baby for adoption, a connection between the siblings still exists and needs recognition. Learn how the prospective adoptive family plans to identify the relationship between the children. Some adoptive parents stick with "brother or sister" while others feel more comfortable referring to your children as a "birth sister or birth brother." It cannot be overstated how important it will be that you and the adoptive family allow the siblings to remain in contact. It is important that you solidify this arrangement with the family and include it in the contact agreement. This will help your child to deal with the grief and loss of the adoption.

One birthmother describes her five-year-old daughter's reaction to the adoption of her younger sister:

"My daughter knows she has a birth sister and talks openly about it. They have a special relationship. They are full siblings, and we want them to know each other. My daughter seems to accept the adoption. We are committed to keeping their connection intact."

Erika, 24-year-old birthmother

Children take their cues from the adults in their lives who they know and trust. If the grown-ups are relaxed and confident about the nature of the open adoption arrangements, their comfort goes a long way towards reassuring the children that relationships in their family are healthy. Regardless, placing a baby for adoption will be a significant loss for your other children, and they will grieve. Give them wide latitude to express their feelings. Even though it will be difficult to see your children in pain, expressing anger and sorrow may be a normal part of your children's grieving process.

Involving your child in counseling before and after the placement can be enormously helpful. It can alleviate some of the burden you may feel from having to be your child's main support while you are grieving yourself. Talking to other birthparents who have children is another good way to understand and support your kids, and you might not feel so alone.

If you are worried that your other child is unusually depressed, lethargic, or anxious, you should seek professional help immediately. A therapist can assess if your child is in need of further treatment. Most kids will have some emotional reaction, which is normal during times of stress and transition. It is common for them to feel sad and to exhibit some behavioral changes. Please be sure to engage with a professional who understands and supports open adoption as they will understand the therapeutic value of your child having contact with his or her sibling whom you placed for adoption.

Some Common Reactions from Children

- Curiosity (asking lots of questions)
- Regression in skills (such as toileting or eating independently)
- Anger or acting out
- Clinginess
- Acting overly protective of you
- Fearfulness (if you leave, will you return?)
- Apathy (lack of response or reaction)
- Withdrawal or silence
- Sadness
- Unwillingness at times to talk about the baby, the adoptive family, or adoption in general

If You Are an Adoptee

If you are an adoptee, making an adoption plan may be especially meaningful. If you had a positive experience growing up, you may feel empowered to "pay it forward" and give this child the same gift you feel your birth and adoptive parents gave to you.

If you did not have a positive adoption experience, you may be unable to move forward with an adoption plan without a lot of support. Even if you have a lot of people backing your decision to make an adoptive placement, you may feel unable to move forward. In this case, you should consider talking to family members about parenting your child or working on a plan that allows you to parent.

For birthmothers who are adoptees themselves, it can be a very powerful experience to see your baby for the first time because your baby may resemble you in ways no one else in your family does. You may be especially surprised and overwhelmed by the feelings you have after the birth. This is true for all birthmothers, but birthmothers who are also adoptees tell us the intensity is quite strong. Take some time in preparation for your delivery to explore and express your experience as an adoptee with a counselor, if possible.

If You Have Previously Placed a Child for Adoption

If this is your second or third adoption, you may think it will not be as difficult this time. Some birthmothers we have worked with said their second placement was easier because they knew what to expect. Others told us it was much more difficult, perhaps because they revisited the grief from the first adoption or because they felt bad about another unplanned pregnancy.

Rather than making things easier, earlier losses can complicate the more recent loss. A loss is not necessarily something we get good at handling just because we have experienced a lot of them. If you are considering another placement, take time to examine the feelings surrounding your other placement or placements.

Preparing to Say Good-Bye

"No one is ever prepared. It was so hard!"

Verna, 19-year-old birthmother

"I feel I was pretty prepared for the grieving process. I think I knew what to expect."

Geraldine, 20-year-old birthmother

Thinking about saying good-bye to your baby is a hard thing to do ... so hard that many women choose not to think about it at all while they are pregnant. Even if you are planning an open adoption, you are choosing to step out of the role of mother and into the role of birthmother. While that is a very important role in your child's life, someone else will be your child's primary caregiver. This choice means you will most likely not be present for his or her first steps, first words, and other major milestones parents assume they will witness.

Some expectant mothers hope that they can evade the uncomfortable feelings and grief that adoption will cause. Our experience is that the more an expectant mother is able to face these feelings before the birth and placement, the better she is able to handle the feelings when they do come. There is no way to completely avoid the sense of loss that comes after the delivery, but working with a counselor to anticipate what you might feel can help you manage the grief and help you move through it.

Here are some things that you can do to help yourself through the difficult period after the birth:

- Make a list of the reasons you are making the adoption plan. Keep it in your hospital bag so you can refer to it at difficult moments.
- Ask your counselor, a friend or a family member to stay with you after you deliver so you can talk openly and freely about what you are feeling.

- Keep a journal during your pregnancy and after your delivery.
- Plan some ways to pamper yourself.
- Write a letter to your baby during your pregnancy and postpartum period, describing what you are feeling and thinking.
- Create an action plan of the goals you want to accomplish in the years after the placement.
- Write a letter explaining why you chose adoption that you will eventually give to your child when he or she is older.

CHAPTER 6: HOSPITAL AND BIRTH

My hospital experience was very positive. I had my own room for labor and delivery, which was very helpful. The nurses were good to me and made me feel comfortable. All of the nurses and my doctor knew of my decision and respected my wishes. It was important to me that my delivery room could accommodate a big group. When my son was born, there was a full house. My stepmother was my labor coach, along with my boyfriend, whom I met when I was three months pregnant. My father was holding my hand. The adoptive family and their daughter were in the delivery room, too. Finally, the doctor and nurses were very supportive. It was a wonderful experience for all of us, as well as a very special bonding time. I wouldn't change anything about my hospital experience."

Laura, 18-year-old birthmother

"I wish I hadn't played 'ostrich' throughout my pregnancy."

Marielle, 29-year-old birthmother

"It was short and scary!"

Jessica, 15-year-old birthmother

Some women wait until the last minute or make no plans at all for the birth, while others have very detailed and specific ideas about their birthing experience that they include in their birth and hospital plans. The choices about labor and delivery are yours. Even if you developed a hospital plan, you can change those choices at any time, including during the labor and birth. It is a good idea to have a coach or other designated advocate to relay your wishes during your delivery.

Labor and Delivery

"My baby ended up being born three weeks late, and I started labor the morning I was induced. There was a wonderful nurse at the hospital that spent most of the night just visiting with me before she had to go off duty. She left before the baby was born, but I had shared with her that the one thing I really wanted was a Butterfinger. When I went back to my room after the delivery, I found one on the table next to my bed. I was able to spend three days with my little girl before placing her with the adoptive family. It was great."

Rosemarie, 22-year-old birthmother

The birth of your baby, while a miraculous event, may be very different from what you expected. Even though you wanted to have friends, family, and/or the adoptive family at your bedside, you may decide to ask people to leave. You may end up having an unplanned Caesarean section or you might request an epidural because the pain is greater than you anticipated. You might have a very short labor and deliver before the adoptive family or your support people can make it to the hospital (especially if they are coming from a distance), or you might be in labor for a very long time. Being prepared for any situation will ease your distress or frustration if your labor is not exactly what you hoped.

"I was dead tired from being in labor all night without sleep, I had no idea what to expect, and I HURT!"

Annie, 33-year-old birthmother

"I had a long labor, but after I received my epidural block, I had no pain and delivered my daughter with no problems. I was awestruck by the whole ordeal; I didn't talk much and watched everything with very large eyes. It was much less terrifying than I was expecting it all to be."

Jackie, 27-year-old birthmother

What If My Baby Has a Problem?

Most deliveries are difficult but "normal," meaning the baby and the mother have no serious medical complications. A small percentage of births, however, result in serious problems for the mother and/or baby. In these situations, the most critical issue is the health and safety of the mother and baby. Everyone's energy needs to remain focused on this until both are medically stable.

If the baby is born with serious medical problems or a genetic defect, all parties may need to reassess their plans. It is critical to discuss the issue of a disability before the delivery so you are aware of the adoptive family's willingness to proceed with the adoption if baby should have any special needs.

This is a topic that the adoption counselor should raise during the match meeting. The scope of the problem or disability may not be immediately clear if, for instance, the baby has a respiratory problem. Other problems, such as Down's syndrome or a cleft palate, may be more readily identified. You and the prospective adoptive family will need to regroup and discuss your options after you have recovered from the delivery.

While some potential adoptive families will make a commitment to adopt your baby no matter what the circumstances, many are reluctant to adopt a severely disabled baby. If the prospective adoptive family chooses not to move forward, you will need to make a number of decisions. For example, will you parent the baby yourself, or will you want to select another adoptive family?

These unexpected circumstances may leave you too distraught to decide immediately. There are agencies that specialize in special-needs adoptions and if you decide to move forward with your adoption plan, your counselor can connect you with those resources. Although you will probably be exhausted and extremely stressed, it is important to ask for help during this time. It is also important for you to take all the time you need to assemble your support team and to consider all your options.

If your baby has medical problems and needs to remain in the hospital after your discharge, you have the right to visit as much or as little as you like. Leaving the baby in the hospital may complicate any feelings of guilt and bewilderment you have. Your counselor is a crucial resource for you and the adoptive family during this period, not only to give support, but also to help solve problems.

Spending Time with Your Baby

"After I had the baby, I was still trying not to think about it because I was so tired and sore that crying aggravated everything. I felt like I was being torn apart. My heart felt like a thousand tiny glass shards."

Roxanne, 16-year-old birthmother

"I felt so very heartbroken, even though I knew it was still for the best. The fact that he has the very best parents (and a wonderful birthmother and sisters) makes the pain subside and overcomes all the darkness and emptiness I feel."

Agnes, 22-year-old birthmother

"The first day was filled with awe and excitement. It was the second day that the sadness kicked in. I knew that all of my reasons for choosing adoption were solid, but as my heart began to betray me, those reasons seemed to get a bit fuzzy."

Ellen, 30-year-old birthmother

Countless birthparents tell us they never imagined the joy and the pain they would feel after the birth of their child—joy from the extraordinary experience of seeing their baby for the first time, and pain from knowing they will have to separate from the baby. Women who never wanted to parent find themselves falling in love with their baby.

You may need more or less time in the hospital with your baby than you had originally planned. A change in plans after the birth does not necessarily mean a change of heart about your adoption plan. While some women fear that spending time with the baby in the hospital will make separation unbearable, spending time with your baby may also reconfirm your adoption decision.

"I was able to spend two days with my son after he was born. They were two of the most important days of my life. He was so tiny and precious. I spent time just looking at him."

Alicen, 23-year-old birthmother

"The adoptive mother stayed in the room with us overnight. I was able to watch her get up with him, feed him, and cuddle him back to sleep. We talked a lot that night; it was a really special experience."

Keisha, 29-year-old birthmother

You may hear a lot about bonding during this time. The prospective adoptive family might be fearful that if you "bond" with your baby, you might not be able to place him or her for adoption. However, you already have bonded with your baby during your pregnancy. Being with your baby after delivery will help you to reconfirm or reconsider your decision.

Some women are clear that they do not want to spend time with their baby at all, and that is a legitimate choice. Many women also report that watching the adoptive parents interact with the baby reaffirms their commitment to the adoption.

Some women choose not to spend time with their baby in an attempt to decrease the sense of loss after the placement. In reality, there is no way to avoid the grief process, and spending time with the baby and the adoptive parents gives you the opportunity to create memories to attach your feelings to later on.

Remember that the hospital plan is simply a plan. It is not a contract and can be altered at any point. The hospital personnel and adoptive parents should be respectful of any changes you decide to make.

Your hospital stay may be very brief: twenty-four to forty-eight hours for an uncomplicated vaginal delivery and two to five days for a Caesarean section. If you think you need more time with your baby before discharge, here are some alternatives:

- If it can be justified on medical grounds some hospitals may allow a bit more time. Talk to your doctor to see if this is a possibility.
- You may want to spend the night in a hotel with your baby and the birthfather, a close friend or a family member.
- You may decide to take your baby home for a day or two before placing him with the prospective adoptive parent(s).

For the most part, birthmothers feel comfortable sending their baby home with the family they have chosen. However, if you do feel strongly conflicted, take the time you need before the momentous step of placing your baby. While some birthmothers limit the amount of time they spend with their baby in the hospital and report feeling content and satisfied, one of the most common comments we hear from birthmothers is that they wish they had spent more time with their babies.

Making the Transition to the Adoptive Family

Your hospital stay is not only a time to spend with your baby; it is also a time to make the transition to the adoptive family.

Seeing the adoptive family with your baby gives you a chance to assess how it feels to see them together. Some birthparents choose to be the primary caretakers of their baby during the hospital stay, while others choose to share in the caretaking or let the adoptive family take the lead in caring for the baby. Allowing the adoptive family time with the baby is a way you can show your trust and confidence in them. It will also give you the chance to witness the beginning stages of their bonding with the baby they will soon be parenting.

"Watching the adoptive parents fall in love with her was like witnessing the family I created for her take shape in front of my eyes. It was a powerful reminder as to why I was making this choice."

Tonya, 43-year-old birthmother

This is an emotionally charged time for the adoptive family. It is often the culmination of years of highs and lows, perhaps including infertility treatments and unsuccessful attempts to adopt. Adoptive families are sometimes uncertain about how they should express their feelings. They fear that if they are overly expressive, or involved with the baby, they may offend you. However, if they back off too much emotionally, you may think they are not excited or committed to the adoption.

Remember that they are also experiencing an enormously significant event and may not know exactly how to express their feelings. Being able to communicate with each other during this highly emotional time is of the utmost importance. For example, reassuring the adoptive family of your commitment to them and your confidence in their parenting will go a long way towards strengthening your relationship.

Dealing with Others during Your Hospital Stay

"My hospital stay was very relaxed. I felt like everyone was supportive, including the adoptive family, and they understood that

I didn't need any extra stress. The hospital staff was respectful and supportive."

Linda, 21-year-old birthmother

"I can describe my time in the hospital in two words: absolutely horrifying. The nurses were sarcastic, and the doctor was dismissive. If I had known what it was going to be like, I would have done the whole thing at home with a midwife."

Dede, 17-year-old birthmother

During your hospital stay, your friends and family members may be involved and want to visit, participate, or give advice. Think about choosing an advocate during this time—someone whose only mission is making sure everyone is responding appropriately to your needs, and who can communicate your wishes to others.

Conflicts can occur with any of the following people:

The Prospective Adoptive Family

They may make a comment that sounds hurtful, even though it is not their intent. Calling your baby "my baby" in front of you, not checking in with you before holding, feeding, or changing the baby, or asking their family to visit without your permission are some examples of things the prospective adoptive family may do that may irritate or even anger you.

Communication is key during this time. If you think the prospective adoptive family is being insensitive, talk to them, or ask your advocate to talk to them. Most prospective adoptive families are sincerely concerned about your feelings. If someone tells them that their behavior is upsetting, they will stop it.

The Birthfather

For many birthfathers, meeting the baby for the first time breaks through any denial they may have been experiencing. His physical resemblance to the baby and the strong feelings that baby evokes may cause the birthfather to reconsider his decision. There have been occasions where the birthfather did not participate in the adoption planning, yet he came to the hospital after the birth. This may also be the first time the birthfather meets the prospective adoptive family, which can be awkward for all involved.

If the birthfather is present the hospital personnel may ask him to put his name on the birth certificate or he may ask to do so. In many states this elevates his rights so that he has as much say as the birthmother about an adoption plan. If possible, you or the adoption social worker should to talk to him about this, and all of his rights, before the birth.

Your Relatives and Friends

It might be wise to talk beforehand with friends and relatives who will be coming to visit you to educate them a little about open adoption and let them know about your hospital plans. This is a time when you need a lot of support and encouragement, rather than entertaining or caring for the needs of others. You may just want to hold your baby or take a nap.

Even though they mean well, your family and friends may make comments that cause you distress, such as "Your baby is so cute! I don't know how you can give him away" or "Are you sure you should be spending so much time with her? It is just going to make it harder to give her up."

Your family and friends may feel overwhelmed by their own feelings. Your parents may have intense feelings when seeing you in emotional pain. In addition, they will feel some deep grief for the grandchild they are losing. Although many adoptive families welcome birth grandparents to remain in touch with the baby as part of the open adoption, there is no legal requirement to include extended families.

Doctors, Nurses, Social Workers, Roommates

If you toured the hospital before your delivery, you will have had the opportunity to meet some of the hospital staff. Most hospitals appreciate knowing about your plans beforehand so the staff understands your needs. Hopefully, the people helping you during your hospital stay will be sensitive and caring. We have heard, however, about well-meaning hospital staff or hospital roommates who made insensitive comments or questioned some birthmothers' choices.

If you suspect that rooming with another mother and baby will make you feel uncomfortable, you should talk to your doctor or the medical social worker in advance to try to arrange a private room. Your adoption counselor will also be in communication with the hospital and can see what the room assignment protocol is in these situations. Most hospitals will be able to accommodate a request for a private room when a woman is making an adoption plan, but some will not.

Leaving the Hospital

"I video-recorded a good-bye to Jeff after he was born. I held him, and said why I was doing this, and told him I loved him. It was very healing."

Theresita, 25-year-old birthmother

If you are placing your baby with the adoptive family when you leave the hospital, it will be a momentous time. You will be saying farewell to your baby as his or her mother. You have been with him or her for the last nine months, and, even though it felt at times like this day would never come, when it finally does, you may wish it had not.

You are in the midst of a role change. You are no longer mother but birthmother. As much as you have prepared for this day, you may not feel ready for the enormity of the feelings. You may be physically uncomfortable and emotionally drained, so this is not the time to be shy about asking for help. Some birthparents ask the adoptive family to take them home and spend time with them and the baby after leaving the hospital.

Depending on the state and type of adoption (agency or attorney), you will most likely have to sign some paperwork before leaving the hospital. At the very least, you can anticipate signing a form that allows the adoptive family to make medical decisions for the baby until he or she is legally theirs.

Make sure you thoroughly understand any papers before you sign them. You can have an attorney review any document before signing it. If you are working with an adoption social worker, she will have already reviewed with you any expected paperwork before your discharge from the hospital.

Ceremonies

Some birth and adoptive families prepare and participate in rituals or ceremonies to honor the new family they are creating. This can be done at the hospital or any time after leaving. A ceremony can be spiritual or not, and it can occur in a house of worship, a hospital chapel, a park, your home, the adoptive family's home, or any place that has significance for you.

The following are examples of ceremonies you may choose to use:

- Everyone lights a candle and makes a wish for the baby and for each other. The birthparents light the candle first. Then they pass it on to the adoptive parent(s).
- The adoptive family and birthparents plant a tree in a location where the child can witness it grow over the years. The tree can symbolize the beginning of life and the promises made to each other that day.
- A minister, rabbi, priest, imam, spiritual advisor or friend reads a meaningful passage or says a prayer for the baby, the adoptive family, the birthparents, and their families.

- A birth and/or adoptive family member read a special poem or sing a song.
- Some houses of worship have dedications for adopted babies, in which the birthparents and adoptive family participate.
- The adoptive family and birthparents read letters to each other and to the baby. The letters usually include their hopes and dreams for the child's future and for the future of their relationship with each other. If the adoptive family or birthparents are already parenting other children, it can be a meaningful and healing experience for those children to also participate in the ceremony.

Terminating Your Rights

You will retain legal rights to your child until you sign a relinquishment, surrender, or consent to adoption. Agencies require a relinquishment or surrender, while attorney adoptions require a document called the consent to adoption. Regardless of the type of adoption, you cannot terminate your parental rights until after the birth. Some states allow the birthfather to sign forms allowing the adoption to proceed before the birth, but the birthmother may only sign a consent, relinquishment, or surrender after the birth. Please note some states require you to sign documents terminating your rights in the hospital.

We think it is very helpful to review all the consent, relinquishment or surrender paperwork before the birth of your baby. The language in the forms can sound quite harsh, particularly if you are reading it for the first time after the birth of your baby, and if you live in a state where you will be required to sign documents terminating your parental rights in the hospital. Reviewing the paperwork with your attorney or counselor will familiarize you with the language at a time when you may be less emotional and able to process the information more easily. It also gives you time to think of any additional questions before signing the documents.

A Change of Heart

After the birth of your baby, your emotions and love for the baby may overwhelm you, and you may find yourself reconsidering your decision to place your baby. Most birthparents go through a time when they reconsider their decision, especially after the birth; this is normal. If you are having doubts about your decision, talk to someone you trust. You might be getting pressure from everyone around you, but it is crucial to think about what is best for you and your baby.

Some of the questions and issues to consider if you are reconsidering your adoption plan are:

- Since you made your original adoption plan, has anything changed in your life that makes parenting a better option?
- What is in the best interest of your baby?
- Will there be support for you if you choose to parent this baby?
- If the birthfather is now encouraging you to parent, you need to consider if it is a good decision for you and your baby.
- Can you make a decision now, in a very short time that will undo the plan you have been working on for many months?

If your change of plans is solely because of the intense feelings that have surfaced since your baby's birth, you might want to take time to sit with your feelings. Some birthparents come close to changing their mind because the grief is so overwhelming, making it hard to think clearly.

"I almost didn't go through with it. The grief was so painful and I just wanted it to stop. I had to remember that I'm doing this for my baby and that it wasn't going to feel like this forever."

Shonda, 23-year-old birthmother

*"My decision to place my baby for adoption was made on
sound reasoning. Though after her birth I would have loved to
parent her, I knew nothing in my life or circumstances had
changed, and I still could not give her the things I desired for her,
except by placing her into her parents' home. What I did not
anticipate was the love I would feel for her parents and the great
longing I had to put my arms around them and say thank you."*

Alice, 18-year-old birthmother

If you are reconsidering your decision, which is a valid
choice, you need to inform the prospective adoptive family. If you
feel unable to talk to them alone, you might want to ask your
counselor, the social worker at the hospital, or a trusted friend to
help you. Most adoptive families are incredibly anxious during this
time, and if you are really changing your mind, it is only fair to let
them know as soon as possible.

Changing Your Mind after the Placement

*"I knew the adoption wasn't right for me after I had Alex
and he went home with his family. I couldn't go on with my life . . .
I got Alex back after one month, but through the whole month, it
never got any easier."*

Helena, 20-year-old mother

Although most women who make an adoption plan follow
through with their original intent, there are women who cannot,
and they ask for their baby back after the placement. The reasons
these women change their mind about the placement are as varied
as the women themselves, but a common theme is "I didn't know it
would be this hard."

Changing your mind after the placement will be difficult
for you and devastating for the adoptive family, to say nothing of

the disruption for the child. It is something to examine fully when making your original plan.

We always ask women before the birth, "What would cause you to change your mind about your adoption placement?" and we usually hear, "Oh, I could never do that! This is what I want. I would never do that to Joe and Mary!" We are convinced that most birthmothers who change their minds do not do it to hurt the adoptive family. They just were not prepared for the intense emotions and grief that follow a placement.

The most common time during which a birthmother changes her mind about adoption is in the hospital and during the first month after the birth. A much smaller percentage of birthmothers, however, decide they want their child back several months after the placement, assuming they have not terminated their parental rights.

Another contributing factor to birthmothers changing their minds is a deteriorating relationship with the adoptive family. One birthmother who asked for her child back describes her situation:

"I picked the prospective adoptive family because they seemed to share my values, but they were really controlling during my pregnancy, even making disparaging comments about what food I ate. I decided that was not a big enough issue to stop the adoption, but after the placement they constantly made excuses about why they could not see me. I finally realized they did not intend to keep their commitment for an open adoption. After they canceled our second scheduled visit, I knew this would not work for me. I told the adoption counselor I wanted the baby back. Then I chose another family and we made an adoption plan that we all agree is working well. Even, now, five years later, I know I made the right decision."

Catherine, 31-year-old birthmother

While there can be feelings of jealousy and resentment toward the adoptive family following a placement, if you find that

113

you are angry all the time and unable to talk to the adoptive family, you should call your counselor. Sometimes minor misunderstandings can blow out of proportion in the very sensitive post-placement period. A session to discuss hurt feelings is often helpful during this critical time.

We have worked with birthmothers and adoptive families who have been able to resolve these conflicts and move ahead with their adoption plan. We have also been involved in adoptions where the birthparents decided that placement was not the right option and then decided to parent their child. If your counselor is truly objective and sensitive to you and the adoptive family, she will be able to help you sort through your feelings and come to a decision that is right for you.

If you have already placed your baby with the adoptive family but are sure you want your baby back, you need to talk to your counselor immediately about how you are feeling. Sometimes just voicing your feelings will help you recognize the grief and sorrow associated with your loss. Most birthparents go through a time when they think they want their baby back, even if they do not tell anyone. Some birthmothers have told us that at this point it can be helpful to talk to the adoptive family or visit them and the baby.

"I just kept having dreams of my baby crying. I would wake up and think he was crying because he missed me, or because the family did not love him as much as I did. I just thought about him night and day. I decided to go visit. I really thought that maybe I would be taking him home that day, but I didn't tell anyone. The visit was hard, but I just knew I couldn't take him back. It wasn't about my being afraid of hurting his adoptive family, but I just realized that he was as happy with them as he would be with me. They loved him completely, and I could see him any time I wanted to. I was still sad but relieved to be out of such turmoil."

Andrea, 19-year-old birthmother

If you decide to ask for your baby back, there are issues to consider:

- What is the legal status of your adoption?
- Who will tell the adoptive family? You? Your counselor?
- When will the adoption provider return the baby to you, and under what circumstances?
- Will your family be involved?
- Is the birthfather aware that you are going to parent your baby? Is he supportive?

As difficult as it may seem, in most cases it is best if you talk to the adoptive family about your plans to parent your child. If you have been working with a counselor, the counselor can be the one to initially tell them what your plans are, but it can be incredibly healing if they also hear from you.

When an adoptive family returns a baby, we suggest a joint meeting between the birth and adoptive family at a neutral location with one or two counselors and support people. These meetings can be very emotional and intense, but they are incredibly important for healing. The adoptive family is always deeply sad and often angry because they feel betrayed. The birthmother probably feels a tremendous amount of guilt and sadness, mixed with relief. Both parties need a counselor present so they can express their feelings without things getting out of control.

In preparing for this meeting, try to remember that while there is sure to be anger, you can help the adoptive family with the emotional process of moving through their pain just by your willingness to be present for a part of it. This may facilitate their ability to go on and eventually find success adopting another baby.

If You Do Change Your Mind

- Be truthful, open, and honest about your reasons for now wanting to parent.

- Be compassionate. The adoptive family will need understanding and compassion as they give up a child they have loved as their own.
- You do not have to apologize for your decision to take your baby back, but consider expressing your sorrow at causing the adoptive family pain. If it is true, reassure them that your decision had nothing to do with them. Let them know that you could not have picked a better family, but that you simply could not live without parenting your own child.
- Be thankful. Thank them for being such great parents and for loving your baby.
- Let them grieve. Be willing to listen to them express their feelings about losing the baby that they thought would be theirs. An adoption counselor can provide safety and structure for this expression of feelings.

"I am sorry that I hurt this wonderful family, and I regret missing the first month of my son's life. The only good thing is that instead of being forced to raise my son, it feels that I've chosen to."

Helena, 20-year-old birthmother

CHAPTER 7: GRIEF, LOSS AND HEALING

"I never knew I could hurt so much. I never thought I would cry so long."

Loni, 14-year-old birthmother

The loss of a child, no matter how that loss has come about, brings very profound pain and sadness. The first few days or even weeks after you place your child with his or her new parents might be the saddest and most painful you have ever experienced.

Sometimes the sadness does not come right away. Some women consciously try not to feel the loss until they have achieved some distance from it—sometimes waiting until they can no longer change their minds about the placement. Other women, busy in their lives, keep telling themselves they do not have time to think about it. Still others are afraid to feel the sadness for fear they will feel it too deeply and will not be able to recover. Of course, many birthmothers simply surrender to their feelings and cry a lot until they begin to feel relief.

Adoption involves loss for each member of the adoption triad. For adoptive families, the loss lies in the absence of the idealized birth child, the loss of their bloodlines, and the loss of privacy and control. The adoptee loses the chance to grow up in his or her original family and often his or her original culture. For the birthmother, the loss is easy to see—losing a child that you conceived, carried within your body, and brought into this world.

Grief is an emotion that we as a culture find uncomfortable. We dislike feeling sad, and we have a hard time knowing how to help those who are mourning. Nevertheless, grief is one of the most common emotions. Everyone experiences loss. Loss comes in many forms, from relatively small losses like losing a ring you treasured because it once belonged to your grandmother, to the major ones like losing a job, breaking up with your partner or the death of a loved one.

A grieving process accompanies every loss. While we have rituals around death, we do not formally recognize most other losses. This lack of acknowledgement only reinforces the feeling of unreality that surrounds the grieving process of adoption. Traditionally our culture has ignored a birthmother's loss and grief.

Only recently have people begun to understand the importance of grieving such a loss. Historically, adoption workers told birthparents to "move on with your life." Placing a child for adoption was regarded in society as a positive outcome to an unfortunate situation. There was often an assumption that the results for the birthmothers were positive and that there was little, if any, need for post-placement counseling for birthmothers.

Fortunately, this situation has changed significantly, as birthmothers have become more vocal about their needs and about the long-term effects of unresolved grief. Most adoption agencies are now very sensitive to the issue of post-adoption loss and train their counselors in grief counseling. There are also therapists who work with birthmothers and understand the issue of post-placement bereavement.

Everyone grieves in her own way. There really is no right or wrong way to grieve, and no prescription to make the pain go away. Grief has a way of taking its own path, but it is part of the recovery process. In fact, grief is such a universally experienced emotion that researchers have studied it extensively. Psychiatrist

Elizabeth Kübler-Ross's well-known theory identifies five themes or "stages" of grief and loss:

- Denial
- Anger
- Bargaining
- Sadness/Depression
- Acceptance/Resolution

Denial

Simply stated, this is the stage where you consciously or unconsciously refuse to accept the reality of what is happening because it is too painful and you are not ready to face the hurt. The numbness you may feel after the birth is a normal response to the loss you are experiencing. Some people experience this physically as a lack of feeling or detachment — almost as if you were in another body or another world. You may think, "This is a dream — I'm really going to wake up soon." Denial, if it keeps you from necessary action, can be detrimental. However, denial also helps you because it can temporarily protect you from emotions that are too strong for you to handle. Similar to having an emotional anesthesia, denial can temper painful feelings from crashing down on you all at once and instead let you process the emotions at a tolerable pace.

Anger

Once a person moves past denial, anger is often the next emotion. Anger is a sign that you are starting to take in the reality of the situation. Some people focus anger internally, which sometimes results in hurting oneself through dangerous acts and risk-taking behavior. Other people direct their anger toward family, friends, the adoptive family, your counselor or lawyer, or the birthfather.

People express anger in healthy and unhealthy ways. Anger or rage is a natural reaction to resisting reality, but it is also an emotion filled with power and energy. Anger can be seductive because unlike the numbness of denial and the ache of sadness, it is a feeling full of intensity and force. Anger can propel us towards dealing with the situation and is, therefore, a movement toward health.

Bargaining

This goes something like, "Please God, if you would let me have the money and support I need to raise my child by myself I will never have sex again." While bargaining is a recognition of reality, it also involves a sort of grasping-at-straws desperation, based on the hope that maybe it could be different with divine intervention. It is an attempt to change or alter the outcome of events and can involve some obsessive thinking about the past. Bargaining is a way, albeit temporary, to delay the inevitable sadness which usually follows.

Sadness and Depression

Once the fireworks of anger have subsided, the embers of sadness remain. Sadness is an acknowledgment of the permanent change in your life—the beginning of an understanding that you cannot have things the way they used to be ever again. Depression and sadness can take many forms, physically and emotionally. Interspersed with the sadness may be intense feelings of guilt — that you didn't consider all your options more carefully or that you chose adoption because you had certain goals you wanted to pursue at this time of your life (e.g. school, career, parenting your other children).

Sadness is usually the most difficult part of the grieving process because it is so hard to endure the painful emotions. It may be the time when you feel the most alone and the time when you most question your decision. Recognizing your grief and accepting your pain without judgment can be your first step toward acceptance.

Acceptance and Resolution

Denial, bargaining, anger, and sadness are all a part of achieving acceptance. Acceptance is the acknowledgment that you have done all you can and that now you must find a way to live your life in order to survive, and yes, to flourish. Acceptance allows people to acknowledge that there are things over which we have no control. Acceptance does not mean that you will never feel sad about your decision. You will feel some poignancy throughout your life about having placed your child for adoption. However, you will also experience a new sense of peace and hope as you adjust to your loss.

Physical, Emotional and Behavioral Reactions to Loss

When people talk about grieving, they are often referring to the sad feelings that accompany a loss. Grief reactions, however, can include physical and behavioral symptoms in addition to the emotional ones. Remember that grief is a normal response to an "abnormal" situation, and may have physical symptoms too. Some of the more common symptoms of grieving include:

- Confusion, disorientation, forgetfulness
- Difficulties with concentration and focus
- Excessive worry
- Sleep disorders, recurring dreams or nightmares
- Extreme exhaustion, even if you are getting enough sleep
- Changes in appetite
- Increase in smoking, alcohol or drug use
- Difficulty making decisions
- Clouded judgment
- Numbness and inability to express your feelings
- Mood swings (from euphoria to depression)
- Irritability, resentment, frustration, anger
- Anxiety and panic
- Apathy, isolation, loneliness, vulnerability
- Headaches, dizziness, muscle aches, stomachaches

- Conflicts with people in your life
- Keeping excessively busy to avoid feelings

While any of these reactions can be in response to grief and mourning, you should always consult a doctor about physical symptoms.

Doubts, Behaviors and Paranoid Thoughts that Prove You are a Normal Birthmother

During the time after you place your child for adoption, you will feel many emotions: doubt, guilt, happiness, fear, hope, sadness, shame, listlessness, self-retribution, relief, and confusion. In addition, you will have many questions: What can I expect to feel afterwards? How long will I hurt? What do other birthmothers feel? Is it normal to feel so angry? What does it say about me if I feel happy and relieved? Will I ever stop thinking about my child? Am I having a nervous breakdown?

Most birthmothers ask these questions. In order to help you make some sense of how you might feel, we have put together a timeline describing some characteristic grief reactions during the first year. Grieving is not a linear progression; you will go back and forth through the stages and may have a day where you find yourself feeling like it is the first week when it is the sixth month. The intensity of your feelings will ebb and flow as life progresses and you will experience and re-experience many of the feelings described below.

We hope you will be able to locate yourself somewhere on this list—but do not worry if your feelings are not exactly under the specified week or month. The most important thing about your recovery is that, overall, you should feel like you are moving forward. The recovery timeline describes a spiraling process, not a straight line. Please note it is only a guide.

Grief Responses During the First Year

The First Week:

- You are overwhelmed with love for your baby.
- Crying every day is typical.
- You ache for the baby to be with you.
- You have obsessive thoughts about the baby missing you.
- You worry constantly that the baby is not okay.
- You are numb, tired and hurt all over.

If you find yourself having thoughts about hurting yourself or others, you may be experiencing postpartum depression. If you think you are suffering from postpartum depression, please see a doctor immediately. Postpartum depression is a serious illness, but there are treatments that will help.

The First Six Weeks:

- Random crying jags—anything will set you off.
- You feel like a part of you is missing.
- You notice lots of babies and children; all the movies on TV seem to be about children and adoption.
- You feel different about many of the people you used to feel comfortable around; they seem immature or superficial.
- If you have a tendency toward alcohol or drug abuse, you may feel a craving for overdoing it.
- You may reevaluate your decision to place your baby.
- You may begin to second-guess your choice of adoptive family. Why do you think you know them or can trust them?
- Feelings of great sadness, heaviness, fatigue, anxiety, irritability; sleep disturbances are common.
- You try to move forward, but all the plans you once looked forward to do not sound as good anymore—you forget why you chose adoption.

- You also feel relief and elation at your accomplishment—you feel proud of yourself.
- You hold on to thoughts of your baby.

By Three Months:

- You still feel sadness and think of the baby often, but the intensity of the sadness is lessening.
- You cry, but not indiscriminately, and only in reaction to something triggering a vulnerability.
- Your body is starting to recover and you have more energy.
- If you have contact with the adoptive family and baby, the pictures or visits can create conflicting emotions.
- You are beginning to feel some optimism about the future and hold out some hope that you will be OK.
- Just as you feel a little more stable, you approach the anniversary of the time when you got pregnant, which brings back many memories and could trigger feelings of hopelessness.
- As you start to heal, you may experience feelings of guilt.

By Six Months:

- Some time goes by (this could be a minute, an hour or a day) and you notice you have not thought about the baby—you wonder if you are forgetting about him or her.
- If you are still experiencing intense sadness, you might wonder if there is something wrong with you, especially if you are around people who are uncomfortable with your pain.
- You are feeling some periods of acceptance interspersed with the sadness.
- Your sadness is no longer a stranger to you and the pain feels a little softer.
- You might even find yourself laughing or wanting to go out with your friends, something you could not even imagine doing a few months ago.

At One Year:

- On the baby's first birthday, you remember all you have experienced.
- You may feel anger, sadness, regret and/or depression with a severity you had not expected.
- You are aware that you will never be the same.
- You are starting to get your life back and think about the future.

Moving through Your Grïef toward Acceptance and Healing

The grieving process does not magically come to a halt at the end of the first year. Grief counselors say that grieving continues well beyond the first year and that a prolonged grief response to a difficult loss is not abnormal. The first year is significant, though, because for many it is the most intense.

The first year after placement, you will have experienced all the important anniversary dates once (i.e. finding out you were pregnant, making your adoption decision, giving birth, placing your baby with the adoptive family, and going through the holidays). You will have achieved some distance and, hopefully, some moments of peace and acceptance.

In the stages of grieving, you probably recognized some of the emotions you experienced during your pregnancy and birth. You may still be going through some of those stages. The grieving process is fluid, and you will drift in and out of different feelings over time. You may experience anger, sadness, or even denial throughout your life. No one moves neatly through these emotions; there is no definite beginning or end. You can expect adoption-related feelings to resurface as you travel through certain passages in your journey of life.

Grieving is hard work. It takes time and patience. It involves paying attention to your emotions, being compassionate toward yourself and accepting your feelings without judgment. By allowing your feelings to exist, you can begin the process of healing. Your experience of healing will reflect your previous losses (and how you mourned them), your upbringing, culture, your life situation, your support system, and your strength. Just as people recover from physical injury at different rates and in different ways, individuals heal from emotional injury in distinctive ways.

Healing faster than the other birthmothers you know does not necessarily mean that you are in denial. Healing more slowly does not mean that you do not want to move forward. Your friends, family and acquaintances may have suggestions or even unsolicited advice about your healing process. However, in the end, you are the one who must be comfortable with the pace of your own recovery. Being able to accept the particular feelings at the time they occur is one of the most important tools in the healing process. If you are feeling sad or angry, guilty or numb, and can acknowledge these emotions, as distressing as they may be, you will find that you are progressing. It is hard to be sad, but acceptance and compassion toward yourself is central to your recovery.

Unresolved Grief

Unresolved grief refers to grief that you repress or deny for a very long time. There is very little acknowledgement of the loss and no movement toward acceptance and healing. This may occur because the loss is extremely intense or painful, and the person has no support or ability to express a range of emotions. Sometimes the person feels afraid and unequipped to handle the enormity of her feelings and suppresses all her painful emotions. Some people fear that if they start crying, they will never stop or that anger is just not an appropriate emotion to express.

No one teaches us how to deal with our grief, and the unfortunate consequence is that people often ignore or push their feelings aside. People hold onto their grief for a variety of reasons and often are not even aware that they are still grieving for a loss that occurred years before. Several losses close together or important losses that people do not grieve can complicate the grief.

Unresolved grief can compromise your life. Suppressed grieving may take the form of anger or blame, physical ailments, addictions, job difficulties or relationship problems. If you feel that you have been unable to express your emotions or that you are stuck in a particular stage of grieving and are concerned that you are not moving forward, see a therapist who specializes in the grief and healing process.

"I felt pretty good throughout the match, but about six weeks after I placed, it hit me. I was struggling with my vacuum cleaner and found myself crying and yelling at it. I called my adoption counselor and told her that I was ready to start dealing with my grief."

Marcie, 21-year-old birthmother

How Do I Know If I Need Help?

There are times when birthmothers find that their lives are not moving forward and that, in fact, they are more depressed than ever. You are the best judge of how you are doing, and what may be normal for someone else may not be normal for you. It is always appropriate to ask a professional—a counselor, psychologist, psychiatrist, or medical doctor—for help evaluating your emotional health. Most likely you will receive reassurance that what you are experiencing is normal and okay. If not, medical or psychiatric intervention may be needed in order to help you over the "humps" of recovery.

When to Ask for Professional Help

- Anytime you feel stuck or unable to move forward in your grieving.
- If you feel like you have no one to turn to for support.
- If, after one month, you are still unable to get dressed and out of the house.
- If, after three months, you still believe you have no future.

- If, after six months, you are still crying every single day.
- Any time you have thoughts of suicide.

Beware of Drugs and Alcohol

If you had a problem in the past with alcohol or drug abuse, the period right after placing your child for adoption is a very fragile time. Sometimes birthmothers use alcohol or drugs to try to dull the pain or elevate their mood. We must caution you about attempting to cope in this fashion.

While drinking or using drugs may temporarily ease your sadness, they only hinder your natural grieving process. Treating your pain through substance use only delays the inevitable and usually makes it worse by creating another problem.

Will I Be All Right Someday?

If you are like the vast majority of birthmothers we have worked with, you will be able to ride out the turbulence of your emotions and move forward with your life. Life is all about change and loss, making decisions and living with the consequences, and being able to move toward a life of peace and fulfillment. You will do all of these things in your own time. Meanwhile, here are some ways to be kind to yourself:

- Allow yourself time to recover. This is true for any healing process. If you push yourself too soon or set up unrealistic expectations, you will only feel worse when you cannot meet them.
- Allow for changes in your life. Many birthmothers expect to return to their old lives immediately. Not all the things they looked forward to doing after the baby—dating, parties, school, a new job, moving—may have the same meaning they once did. In fact, most birthmothers feel they have matured faster than many of their friends and no longer feel they belong in the same crowd. You have

changed. Give yourself time to figure out how the "new you" wants to live life.

- Seek support from friends who will listen without judgment. Take care of yourself by being with friends who will let you talk about how you feel without trying to fix you. You may need to avoid friends who cannot understand. You might even want to give someone you trust—a close friend, your boyfriend, husband, mother, sister, or roommate—the job of running interference for you. They can take phone messages, answer the door for you, and protect you in general from the people you are not ready to see.

- Do not overdo it. Take on one new thing at a time. Some birthmothers feel they have to radically change their life right after placing a child for adoption. This is generally not the time to move, or plunge into wildly unfamiliar territory. It is good to do things that make you feel productive or move you toward accomplishing goals, such as starting back to school or finding a job. Avoid making major decisions or taking on too much at once.

- You just had a baby. As if that were not difficult enough, your body is changing rapidly too. Your breasts are probably sore and leaky, you may have stitches, your abdomen is stretched and saggy, you may have a few more pounds on you than you would like, and on top of all this, your hormones are going crazy. It is no wonder you are feeling out of control.

- Reach out to the adoptive family. Depending on your relationship with the adoptive family and the agreement you worked out with them for contact after the placement, it can be reassuring to hear their voices, see a picture of the baby and find out how he or she is doing.

- Talk to another birthmother. Someone else who has been through placing a child for adoption can be extremely comforting during times when you are feeling down. Your counselor should be able to connect you with an "alumna birthmother," and the online networking site www.birthmombuds.com is a good resource as well.

129

- Seek counseling. Arrange regular counseling contacts after your placement. Sometimes it helps to talk to someone you don't have to explain yourself to, someone you don't have to "be strong for." If you do not already have a counselor, please consider getting one. It is not too late.
- Make yourself do one uplifting thing a day. It may be as simple as painting your toenails fire engine red, renting a movie, taking a walk, or smiling at yourself in the mirror. You will work up to bigger things.
- Nurture your spirit. You could attend a place of worship, meditate or take a yoga class. You could listen to a soothing tape, read something inspirational or just sit in the sun in a place you love and reflect on the beauty of the world.

CHAPTER 8: THE FIRST YEAR

The first year after placing a child for adoption can seem like a lifetime in itself. You will pass through various stages, look at things from different angles, and experience a multitude of feelings. Many birthparents report that they get through their most difficult times emotionally within the first few months, although some take much longer. One's experience of, and response to, the grieving process is very personal, and there is no "right" way that this happens. Grief is one of those feelings that just will unfold naturally, according to your own personal needs.

The first year after placement is a time to be kind and patient with the grieving process. Any attempt to force, deny, hurry, or criticize the grieving will only obstruct the natural healing. Rather than judging yourself as you adjust to your life "post-adoption," it may be more useful to act as your own "gentle witness" by simply observing your feelings or moods without evaluation.

Intertwined with the grieving process, other developments will unfold during your first year after placement. Your relationship with the adoptive family will continue along its course. Immediately after the birth, this relationship may undergo a strong "stress test" on trust. This is especially true when the adoptive family takes the child home from the hospital before your parental rights are terminated. Each state has different requirements regarding when you can sign to terminate your parental rights, and it is essential that you are familiar with all of your state's laws. In most cases however, the adoptive family takes the baby home from the hospital and begins parenting before the baby is legally theirs.

The Shift in Relationship

"I had my baby on December twenty-first, and that made for a pretty depressing Christmas! When I could stop feeling sorry for all that I was missing, I thought about what a wonderful Christmas present I had given my baby—a new family that could provide everything she needed."

Katy, 21-year-old birthmother

No matter how confident and secure you are with the adoption, you will reevaluate your decision before you terminate your parental rights. It is important to remember that many adoptive families come to this place having undergone previous disappointments. No amount of reassurance on your part will completely convince them they do not have to worry about you changing your mind.

However, they need to be realistic—you cannot know how you will really feel about your adoption decision until the child is born and the time for saying good-bye arrives. But they also have to feel free to begin loving the baby without reservation, to feel like his or her parents, from the moment they take the baby home. Their anxiety is not your responsibility, but your response to it can go a long way toward building a trusting relationship. Hopefully, they will also have a trusted counselor with whom they can share their insecurities, so as not to burden you at a time when you are dealing with your own strong feelings.

Similarly, this is a time when the adoptive family should work to build trust in your developing relationship with them. No matter how strongly they communicate their commitment to you and to the openness of your relationship, you may still fear they will lose interest in you once they begin parenting the baby. One of the most difficult realities to adjust to after the birth is the fact that the child will replace you as the focus for the adoptive family.

"In the first few weeks after placing, I realized that I am grieving two losses. I miss the baby but I'm also feeling a void because I'm no longer the center of the adoptive parents' world. I know they are focused on parenting now, and I want them to be putting all of their energy into that, but I didn't realize how much the shift in their attention would affect me."

Desiree, 27-year-old birthmother

This feeling is natural and to be expected, but it can still be painful. It is important for the adoptive family to be sensitive to you and your needs at this time and work with you to help smooth your transition from being the expectant mother to being the birthmother. We highly recommend talking to each other at the match meeting about your respective expectations for the first few months after the birth.

In our experience, contact immediately after the placement can be very reassuring for all concerned. Oftentimes, birthparents will not feel comfortable calling the adoptive family for fear the family will perceive them as "intruding." In reality, they will be very curious about how the baby is doing and how the family is adjusting to its newest member.

The adoptive family will also hesitate to call the birthparents, despite their concern and affection for them, for fear their phone call will "pour salt in the wound" of an already painful situation. In some adoptions, the birth and adoptive families agree that a "transition period" without contact is the best arrangement for all involved. This is a personal decision and is a topic that the adoption counselor should raise at the match meeting. Whatever your decision, it helps to clarify each person's expectations before disappointments or misunderstandings occur.

Rage and Resentment

As we noted earlier, you might start having negative feelings toward the adoptive family, such as rejection or anger. Seeing the baby you carried and loved for nine months in the arms of the adoptive family can evoke very strong emotions, especially in the beginning. The resentment may not make sense to you, especially since you are the one who chose this plan, but it is part of the loss experience. You might ask yourself, "Why do they get to keep my baby? Why are they so prepared financially or emotionally that they are ready to parent? Why not me?"

This is a time in the grief process when birthparents must continue to remember why they chose adoption in the first place— usually for the well-being of the baby. You may ask yourself, "If this is such a good decision, why does it feel so bad?" Birthmothers need to remind themselves that they made a conscious choice: short-term pain for long-term gain as opposed to short-term gain and long-term pain. In other words, they chose tremendous sadness in the present with the belief that, ultimately, adoption would prove the best choice for their child and for themselves.

"Boy, was I a basket case! Before the birth, I just wanted to get it over with and move on with my life. I tried not to think about the baby so I would not get attached. After the birth, I was torn apart. I could not stand seeing them with my son, and I hated them. Everything they said irritated me. I just wanted to hold my son and never let him go. I was so confused."

Taylor, 21-year-old birthmother

"The first time we had a visit after the hospital, I found myself annoyed at little things that the adoptive mother was doing. I wanted her to hold the bottle differently and was irritated that she hadn't put socks on him. The next day my counselor explained that even though I made the conscious decision to place, feeling jealousy toward the adoptive mother can happen at this stage. I'm

so glad I addressed it with my counselor instead of taking my feelings out on the adoptive mother."

Aliyah, 24-year-old birthmother

Trust and Transition

The post-placement period is extremely important in a number of ways. The adoptive family has a natural need for "permission" to begin bonding as a family. You may need some reassurance that they will honor their future agreements with you. Your relationship with the adoptive family will shift as you establish new roles with one another; the friendship and closeness you have been feeling may change shape. Your relationship with the birthfather may go through changes, too, if you have been working together to complete the adoption. Like any ongoing relationship, there will be growing pains as you, the birthfather, the adoptive family, and eventually the child evolve in your relationships with one another.

Pain and Growth

Painful experiences can also be the gateway to growth. In the midst of your great sorrow, you may not believe this. It can be tremendously annoying when well-meaning friends or family members tell you that the adoption is an opportunity to make changes in your life, or that you should be proud of yourself for doing such an unselfish thing.

However, there is some truth to the notion that the most difficult experiences can bring us to a very deep level of insight and reflection. Perhaps sadness allows us to retreat from the intense, hectic pace of our life for a moment and notice things that we did not see before. Perhaps the intensity of loss makes us much more aware of those things in life that we cherish and helps us redefine what is truly important.

Your New Path

"My counselor now tells me that I used to say the grieving was worse than I expected, although I don't remember saying that now. I think I felt better by the third month, but having the opportunity to see Chad and his parents a few times throughout the first year really helped. He looked so happy and well adjusted. Seeing them just reconfirmed that I absolutely made the right choice."

Kelsey, 31-year-old birthmother

"What helped me during the first year, believe it or not, was feeling free to be sad or cry whenever I wanted. In addition, I tried to think of what was best for my little girl. Keeping her in the foreground of my mind was the biggest help."

Margo, 22-year-old birthmother

The first year following the adoption is an opportunity for you to begin regaining some feeling of normalcy in your life. It is a time for you to experiment with different ways of relating to yourself, to others, and to the adoptive family. It may mean returning to school to continue with your educational goals, returning to work, continuing to parent other children, or beginning a new career or relationship.

Many birthmothers use the placement as a turning point in their lives or an inspiration to begin something new. During the first year you will discover whom you can talk to about your experience. When you begin a new intimate relationship you will need to decide how much of your adoption story to share with the new person in your life.

You will be faced with difficult questions like, "What happened to your baby?" and possibly insensitive comments from people who do not support your choice. Your family members will be experiencing their own grief concerning the baby, which can sometimes complicate how you feel. A common feeling among younger birthmothers is that they have grown up very fast. They feel so much more mature than a lot of their friends and begin to feel distanced from them.

"Everything these girls at school talk about seems so stupid, so trivial. It is like they're looking at the world through rose-colored glasses. I keep feeling like there's no going back for me. I can never go back to the way it was before."

Betsy, 17-year-old birthmother

We hope that you will have begun to surround yourself with people who can affirm what you chose to do. The first year becomes a time to discover whom you can really depend on. Remember to bolster your support system around certain holidays like Christmas, Mother's Day, Father's Day, or the baby's first birthday. Anticipate the mood swings that may accompany these times of year.

Am I a Mom or Not?
After the birth and placement of your baby, you may need to redefine your identity. Some birthmothers struggle with the question, "Am I a mom or not?" This is a very personal question and one that every woman will answer differently. Whether you refer to yourself as a mother or not is your choice, but you are certainly your child's birthmother.

A very difficult part of placing a child for adoption is clarifying your role. You are no longer the parent of the child. Part of the grieving process involves relinquishing the role of being a parent. Even birthmothers who initially told us that they did not want to be a mother are often surprised at how strongly this loss of identity affects them.

You can still offer wonderful things to your child as their birthparent, though. It will take some time to sort this out and develop a relationship based on your new role. If you have a trusting relationship with the adoptive family, you can talk about how you see yourself in relation to them and to your birth child.

Contact during the First Year

Contact with the adoptive family and baby during the first year can range from closed to very open. There is widespread agreement among researchers who study adoption that open adoption has the best outcomes for the adoptee, birthparents and the adoptive parents. Most adoptions today include ongoing visits, although birth and adoptive families negotiate the frequency.

When you are thinking about the kind of contact you envision, keep in mind it is the quality of the relationship that is important, not the quantity of visits. Feeling comfortable and clear about your roles with one another is paramount. Getting together should be a positive experience for all, and sometimes this takes some work and time. If the visits feel uncomfortable, you should consult with your counselor for some help in getting back on track or changing the structure. The spirit of openness, not just "open adoption," is the healthy goal.

If the Adoptive Family Won't Honor the Agreement for Contact

If you made a specific agreement for contact with the adoptive family and they are not honoring their commitment, you should contact your adoption professional immediately. There are many reasons why adoptive families might pull back. They might be fearful about you changing your mind if they have not yet finalized the adoption. They may be feeling insecure about your role as they are trying to develop their own roles as parents. They may be getting negative feedback from others about maintaining a relationship with you. They may need a break from their intense relationship with you so that they can settle down and get used to the changes their life is undergoing.

Today many adoption agencies do extensive counseling with the adoptive family to help them with the intensity of the post-placement period, and most adoptive families will remain committed to the relationship with you. A counseling session or two will offer you both the chance to discuss your fears and redefine your agreement. It is important to note that open adoption agreements are legally enforceable in twenty-three states, which means the courts can make the contact mandatory. A court battle, however, is a good way to destroy a relationship, so we would advise trying to work out any differences through any other means before resorting to filing suit in court.

What Happens if You Decide to Stop Contact

Most birthmothers honor their commitment to the open adoption, and stay in contact with the adoptive family, but some decide they cannot do so for a variety of reasons. Some birthmothers find the contact too painful, others have a new partner they have not told about the adoption, or have fallen on hard times and do not want the adoptive family to know about their situation.

Even in the twenty-three states with enforceable open adoption agreements, there is no legal obligation for you to remain in contact with the adoptive family. Although you can sue the adoptive family to enforce the contact agreement, they cannot do the same to you. You may walk away from the contact agreement without any legal consequences.

Nevertheless, it is important to remember that walking away can be devastating for your birth child. Almost every child wants to know their birthmother, and hear you tell them that you love them and why you placed them for adoption. If your birth child never meets you there could be a hole in their heart forever as they try to make sense of their adoption story without any concrete information from you.

If you cut off contact after participating in regular visits the child is likely to believe that he or she did something to cause the rift, no matter how reassuring their adoptive parents are that your decision had nothing to do with them. Children naturally believe that adult behavior is related to their actions even though this is rarely the case. For example, almost all children harbor guilt if their parents divorce even though divorces are always the result of the adult relationships breaking down, and have nothing to do with the children. It is important to communicate with the adoptive family so they can let your birth child know that you have not abandoned him or her, and most importantly, that he or she did not do anything to cause you to stop visiting.

For some birthmothers the contact becomes too painful to endure. If you feel this way it may be time to consider contacting your adoption counselor, even if it is years later. Perhaps you are suffering from residual grief that you still need to process, or have suffered new losses that are triggering these painful feelings. Your adoption counselor may suggest that you take time off from contact with the adoptive family, and can help you to communicate this information to them so your relationship remains intact while you deal with your ongoing grief. Often with some counseling or therapy birthmothers feel ready to resume the relationship with the adoptive family.

Other birthmothers may have fallen on hard times and are too embarrassed to let the adoptive family know about their situation. Perhaps they are homeless, or have gotten into trouble with the law, spending time in jail or prison. The adoptive family and especially your birth child will worry about you if you suddenly stop contact without any explanation. In these situations, it is best to call your adoption counselor and ask her to tell the family what is happening. Most families will understand and offer support if they can. In addition, your counselor may be able to provide you referrals to resources that can help you.

Perhaps the most difficult situation is if you have a new partner or spouse to whom you have not disclosed the adoption. We understand that this can be a painful discussion, especially if you feel that your new partner will judge you negatively for your adoption decision. Again, talking to your adoption counselor is often the best alternative. She can help you to develop a plan for how to present this information to your partner.

The First Birthday

Even if you are happy with your decision and enjoy a satisfactory relationship with the adoptive family, your baby's first birthday can be a difficult day. All the joy and sadness you feel that day may overcome you in a way you had not anticipated.

The anniversary of any loss is a time to revisit the feelings of that experience. You will find yourself thinking a lot about your baby during this period. As birthmother counselors, we sometimes notice a heightened level of anxiety, depression, agitation, anger and self-destructive behavior in birthmothers as the anniversary date approaches. Some women are perplexed about why their emotional health seems to be in a tailspin, until we remind them that their birth child's birthday is coming up.

Some adoptive families choose to include their birthmothers in the baby's birthday celebration. Most open adoption agreements include a section about how birthparents will be included in the baby's first birthday. But even if you do not formally celebrate your child's first birthday with him or her and the adoptive family, there are many ways to mark the passage of the first year.

Some adoptive families and birthmothers have a small, private party around the birthday. In cases where the birthparents and adoptive family live far from one another, birthmothers can still celebrate the first and subsequent birthdays in a more personal fashion. This could be by taking time for quiet reflection, prayer or meditation or some private outing to symbolize your child's first birthday and your role in his or her life. We definitely recommend some kind of a recognition or affirmation of the adoption, your role as a birthmother, and your birth child.

One adoptive family we know celebrates their child's adoption day (the day the adoption was finalized) with their child's birthparents. Another family celebrates the day they met their child's birthmother because they feel that is the day their child came into their life.

Is Peace of Mind Possible?

Some birthparents report they feel stuck in their pain over the adoption, and time does not seem to be making a difference.

"I kept thinking that my sadness was the only thing I had left connecting me to my daughter—I thought if I began to feel better, I would just lose her again."

Diana, 34-year-old birthmother

"The agony of losing my child has never gotten better. It has been hard for me to continue with my life, and it's already been nine months! Sometimes I wonder if I really made the right decision."

Stella, 20-year-old birthmother

Other birthparents equate recovering and feeling positive with a sense that they have abandoned their child. They think that somehow staying trapped in guilt or sadness is what they should do if they really love their child. Others worry that healing from their grief will bring finality to the adoption process and that this will sever the last connection they feel with their child.

Instead, the opposite is true. Finding pride in your ability to step into the role of "birthmother" is actually the beginning of the lifelong connection you will have with your child. Although difficult to conceive of in the beginning, you are and always will be a very real and important relative to him or her.

You do not deserve to be unhappy, nor would it be healthy for a child to grow up feeling responsible for his or her birthmother's persistent sadness. Your confidence in the decision you made will send him or her the reassuring message that he or she is in the family where he or she is meant to be.

By the end of your first year, we hope you are feeling some acceptance and peace about the adoption. This does not mean you will not feel sad. We hope that one day you can honestly say you do not regret your decision.

A little more than a year after placing her son for adoption, a young woman describes how she has fared emotionally:

"At very first I was really happy and gung-ho on being there and having it really open. After a few months I started to wonder, about what it would be like if I had kept him, and I got a little depressed. Now I am content with the decision I made. I know it was the best decision for everyone involved. I hope to become closer to them than I am right now. I want to be involved in my son's life. I want him to know exactly why I chose what I did and that I still love him no matter what."

Jane, 34-year-old birthmother

CHAPTER 9: BEYOND THE FIRST YEAR

"I am very happy I went through with the adoption. I can see what a great child she is and how great they are as a family."

Makayla, 29-year-old birthmother

"There are days that are still hard for me, and I still feel such sadness."

Lilly, 18-year-old birthmother

"The grieving process . . . I just wasn't prepared for the duration. My son is now three years old, and I am still experiencing the loss and grief. I've never once regretted my decision, but I do miss seeing him. He lives on the other side of the country now, though, so it's a little harder to visit."

Jasmine, 22-year-old birthmother

After the first year, you might expect that your feelings of grief would begin to fade. While it is true that the first year is often filled with sharp, intense pain, regret and longing, the feelings in the subsequent years have been described by some as a dull ache, punctuated by periodic stabs of pain.

For some birthmothers, the awareness that they have given birth to a child and then placed the child for adoption is never far from consciousness. Other women claim that their memories and experiences as a birthmother do not intrude into their thoughts and lives very often, but when they do the women feel surprised by the intensity of their reactions.

By the end of the first year, your life may seem to have returned to some semblance of normalcy. Perhaps you have returned to work or started a new career. You might have taken up where you left off in school or begun a new school program. You most likely will be socializing and having fun with friends and family members. You may be dating or working on improving old relationships. By this time your relationship with the adoptive family is probably more established, and you may be more comfortable with each other.

Maintaining the Relationship with the Adoptive Family

"I have a continually growing relationship with my birth son and his family. I get to visit him a couple of times a year, which is wonderful. His mother is incredible. She sends me, as well as members of my family, all sorts of wonderful things: pictures, letters, and videos of the kids. She is a very thoughtful and loving person. I have the utmost love and respect for them all."

Eva, 35-year-old birthmother

Many adoptive families tell us they feel sad if the birthmother of their child discontinues contact. These same adoptive families may have initially been very reluctant or even scared to have an open adoption, but as they grow to love and care about the birthparents, and are educated about the importance of openness for the child, they are motivated to stay in touch.

It is important to keep your birth child's needs and feelings in mind. If you send a card or a gift, or telephone every birthday and holiday season, for example, your birth child will grow to expect and look forward to this special ritual and may be very disappointed if you decide not to continue the practice. Keeping the relationship up and the communication open in a consistent fashion is very important for your child's sense of continuity and security.

Life throws us curves, of course, and your future may include times when your circumstances do not allow for regular contact. You might be moving frequently, breaking up with a partner, or suffering from an illness. If your birth child and adoptive family are accustomed to hearing from you, it can be upsetting for them if you drop out of sight. A phone call, text, or an email, briefly explaining your circumstances and your need to lay low for a while can assuage their worry. Reassurance that you will again reconnect when you are able is respectful and loving. If the circumstances are more serious (as discussed in Chapter 8) you may want to involve your adoption counselor in these discussions.

Although we emphasize the need for a written open adoption agreement so that there is no confusion moving forward, it is important for adoptive families and birthparents to acknowledge that agreements regarding contact are most helpful when both parties are flexible over time and across differing circumstances. We hope the written agreement enables you and the adoptive family to move forward comfortably, allowing for some flexibility and change as needed.

"I am thankful every day when I think about how lucky my son is to have them as parents. I think I gave him the best gift a mother could give."

Mia, 17-year-old birthmother

Your Personal Life

Your personal life will continue to ebb and flow over the years following the adoption. Your relationship with your own family and the birthfather will most likely change as well. You may notice that you are viewing the world through different eyes after the adoption. It is a maturing and sobering experience: one that most of your friends and acquaintances will not truly understand.

When you talk to your friends and family about your birth child or the adoptive family, they may tell you that you are dwelling on the adoption too much, especially after the first year of the placement. You may hear from people that it is time to "move on" or "snap out of it." Support groups, where you can talk to other birthparents who will listen to and understand your feelings, may be helpful even after the first year of the placement. We have worked with birthparents who periodically "check in" with a support group years after their placement and find it beneficial.

"To see her with them makes me sad at times, but I see their faces, and I smile through the pain. I just wish I could have kept her and raised her, but there are so many reasons why I couldn't. My boyfriend and I try to take one day at a time and concentrate on our goals so that, when the time comes, we will be prepared to have a family."

Hannah, 27-year-old birthmother

Dating and New Relationships

Some birthmothers say the adoption experience has brought them closer to the birthfather, but for others the relationship with the birthfather has ended. Some birthmothers find it difficult to start new relationships because they are feeling raw and do not want to go through another loss if the relationship does not work out. Some worry that a new boyfriend will not understand or accept their adoption decision. They are concerned about introducing a new partner into the adoptive family's life. Others rush into a new relationship because they want to make the sad feelings go away.

Meeting new people or dating can be a positive and healthy experience for you. You do not want to put pressure on yourself to find the perfect partner or your "soul mate," but you might be able to have fun and enjoy life a little more fully. Yes, it probably will be scary. Recognize that you will be vulnerable and be careful not to expect a new romantic relationship to heal the hurt of your loss.

When you feel ready, you owe it to yourself to rejoin friends and have some fun. Test the water as you get to know someone and trust yourself about when it is the right time to share your private matters, including your adoption story.

Pregnant Again?

We have worked with birthparents who become pregnant again relatively soon after their adoption placement. Some birthparents are consciously choosing another pregnancy because they decide they are now ready to parent.

For others however, unconscious motivations are at work. You may be trying to replace the child you have lost. You may be craving the attention you received or the closeness you felt with the adoptive family. You may feel that without being pregnant, your life has no purpose. As much as you may wish to do so, you cannot repeat the experience or replace the child you have placed for adoption. If you find yourself taking sexual risks, reach out to someone you can confide in and whose advice your trust.

If you become pregnant and decide you would like to make another adoption plan, you may want to consider placing your child with the first adoptive family so that your children, whether they are half or full siblings, can grow up together. Many adoptive families will want a sibling placement. Those that cannot accommodate another child will usually agree to stay in touch with the adoptive family with whom you place the new baby so the siblings will know one another. If you are worried about how the adoptive family might react, we suggest you ask your adoption agency or attorney to approach the family.

"I was surprised when our daughter's birthmother called to tell us she was pregnant again less than a year after the placement. I congratulated her, but then she got very quiet and burst out with, 'I want to place this baby for adoption too. Can you take her?' I almost shouted, 'Yes!' and I could hear her start to cry as she said, 'Thank you.' My husband and I are fortunate to now have two beautiful daughters, and to have a close relationship with their birthmother."

Jason, 37-year-old adoptive father

"I really wanted my birth daughter's adoptive mothers to parent my new baby, but I thought it would be too much to ask. Fortunately, the adoption agency said they would talk to them. I was so happy when they said yes. Now both of my birth daughters are together."

Abbie, 28-year-old birthmother

Change in the Adoptive Family

Just as you find your life changing and growing as the years go by, so will the adoptive family. Some changes may be subtle and will not affect you and your relationship with them, but other changes will be major. Some adoptive families decide to adopt a second child, often within two to three years after their first adoption. Not only will this bring another child into their lives, but also it will bring a new set of birthparents. You may be happy for the adoptive family and at the same time feel unsettled and jealous, wondering if their relationship with new birthparents will alter their relationship with you.

Talking to the family about your fears is a good idea. They are probably also worried about having another set of birthparents in their lives and wonder how it will impact their relationship with you. They may also ask your permission to include a photo of you in their adoption letter and online profile. After a contact from a potential birthparent, they may ask you to talk to the "new" birthparents because, after all, who could give them a better recommendation?

Many birthparents are comfortable with such requests, but it is fine to let the adoptive family know if you do not want to participate in the second adoption. Maybe you are shy or the situation just makes you uncomfortable. We encourage you to call your adoption agency or attorney and talk to a counselor if you are having strong feelings.

Some adoptive families have gotten pregnant after adopting their first child. Invariably, the birthparents wonder if the adoptive family will love their biological child more than they love their adopted child. In our experience, adoptive families love their children equally and do not favor one child over the other, although they may love different things about different children, as all parents do.

Another change that may affect your relationship with the adoptive family is moving to a new location. Since we live in a mobile society, chances are that either you or the adoptive family will move one or more times during your lifetime. You may start your relationship living twenty miles from the adoptive family, and five years down the line you may live two thousand miles apart. Although you may not be able to see each other as frequently, your relationship can endure and grow if everyone makes an effort to keep in touch.

If you have an open adoption agreement, especially if it is enforceable by the court, the adoptive family should still be willing to abide by its contact provisions. For example, if the agreement says there will be one in-person visit a year, the adoptive family should make an effort to ensure that the visit happens even if you live across the country from one another.

Change Due to Divorce or Death in the Adoptive Family

Divorce or separation can be an unexpected and upsetting experience for the adoptive family and for you. Adoptive families are not immune to the pressures and difficulties of maintaining a relationship and may decide to separate or divorce. If this happens to your adoptive family, we hope you will be able to maintain a relationship with both adoptive parents. We suggest that before the adoption finalizes, the adoptive family and birthparents commit to each other to stay connected, for the sake of the child, no matter what.

Another extremely difficult experience is a long-term or debilitating illness or death of an adoptive parent. While this is relatively rare, it does happen, and the loss for you and for your birth child will be a big one. The surviving parent will need your support and love during this difficult time.

You and Your Birth Child Through the Years

During your birth child's life, the level of contact may change many times. Your birth child may want different levels of contact with you during different periods of his or her life. It is important that you and the adoptive family maintain a tone of flexibility, always deferring to what is important for the child at any given time. Younger children want to be with their parents most of the time, but as they grow older, they may develop independent relationships with friends and relatives.

Most teens go through conflict with their parents and do or say things to hurt them. This is perfectly normal and it is often the only way they can truly develop a separate identity. An adopted teenager might say to their adoptive parents, "I hate you. I'm going to live with my *real* parents."

This does not mean that you, as the birthmother, should regret your adoption decision or that your child resents you for placing them for adoption. If you are really concerned that that may be the case, you can always discuss it with your child. There is no reason to hold back discussing the adoption with your birth child and his or her feelings about it. One of the most important things you can do for your birth child is to talk openly and honestly about your reasons for choosing adoption.

If you are parenting other children, you can expect your birth child to ask why you chose to place him or her for adoption, but decided to parent your other children. This question may suggest that your birth child feels rejected, but usually he or she just wants the answer. You can confidently tell him or her the truth about the circumstances that led you to choose adoption, and the circumstances that allowed you to parent. Sometimes this includes sharing information that is upsetting, such as the birthfather abandoning you, or unflattering for you, such as having had a drug addiction. Nevertheless, explain that you made the best decision possible considering your circumstances at that time.

Children rarely judge their birthparents. They just want the information. This sort of honesty is one of the best things you can do to enhance your birth child's self-esteem and confidence. It is also imperative that you and the adoptive parents regularly talk to your child about his or her adoption. Do not wait for the child to broach the subject. If you and the adoptive parent or parents regularly bring up the topic your birth child will understand that it is a safe subject and not something they need to feel ashamed or afraid about.

We encourage you to collaborate with the adoptive family about how and when you tell the adoption story to your birth child so you can all agree on what is the best strategy and way to support one another and the child. Keeping open communication and a united front with the adoptive family during this time is important. Offering support and understanding to your birth child, without undermining the adoptive family, is an important role you can play in your birth child's development.

Another thing that you can do to benefit your birth child is to do your part to foster a relationship with the adoptive family that is characterized by respect and integrity. Adoptive parents are human beings with fears, insecurities and vulnerabilities. Respecting their role, devotion and authority with your child will go a long way towards creating a reciprocal relationship.

"The adoption was the best thing that ever happened to me. There isn't a day that goes by that I don't think about my son and how happy he is. It makes me feel happy and confident."

Emma, 24-year-old birthmother

CHAPTER 10: BIRTHFATHERS

Although we wrote this book primarily for expectant mothers and birthmothers, this chapter is devoted to birthfathers and the issues that are particular to them.

Over the last fifty years the American family has changed dramatically as the feminist movement became mainstream, more women went to work, marriage declined as an institution and single men and women chose to parent alone at a rate unprecedented in our history. The word "family" has come to include many different combinations and our schools and cultures reflect these changes.

As women entered the workforce, men became more active as parents. Although change may seem slow in coming and stereotypes persist, there is increasing acceptance of and encouragement for men who want to participate more fully in their children's lives.

This trend is true in the realm of adoption, as well. Until recently, birthfathers were not routinely involved in the adoption planning. They were rarely involved in picking the adoptive family, supporting the birthmother, or witnessing the birth. Adoptive families, birthmothers, and professionals assumed that birthfathers were not interested. However, research, the media and legislation have all begun to reflect the important role that birthfathers increasingly play in an adoption. Whether or not they are still involved with the birthmother, they can be involved in the adoption plan to whatever extent feels most comfortable.

Most adoptive families welcome the inclusion of the birthfather in the adoption planning because they represent half of the medical, cultural and social history of the child. In addition, many children are interested in their paternal birth history and want to connect with their birthfathers as they grow up.

The Birthfather's Legal Rights

The topic of a birthfather's legal rights is a complicated one and is outside the expertise of this book. However, you can certainly get answers to any legal questions regarding your rights and the adoption by consulting an attorney. Adoption attorneys understand birthfathers' rights and are often willing to answer a few questions by phone. If you cannot afford to meet with an attorney, Legal Aid provides low-cost or free legal help in some communities. Adoption agencies will usually answer adoption-related questions without charge over the phone.

State adoption laws are complicated and change frequently. The state where the baby is born usually has jurisdiction over the adoption. Every state government has an adoption unit (sometimes called the Department of Social Services or the Department of Youth, Family and Children), which you can consult regarding questions about adoptions in their state.

The Birthfather's Role

Birthfathers can be husbands, boyfriends, acquaintances, and even "one-night stands." You may find out about the pregnancy at the same time as the expectant mother, at any point during the pregnancy, after the birth of the baby, or even after placement in the adoptive home. You may find out directly from the birthmother, from friends or family, or even by receiving legal papers advising you of the impending adoption.

While the birthmother's connection with the baby is obvious, your involvement may be vague. You may be unclear about what your role is or how you would like to be involved. Many men in this position feel very out of control. Depending on your relationship with the birthmother, you may not have any notion of what will happen next.

When birthfathers first find out about the pregnancy, their initial reaction typically includes numbness and shock; disbelief and denial that the child could be theirs; anger towards the birthmother, themselves, or the universe; and maybe even overwhelming fear.

Your acknowledgement of the situation may happen in stages. The first is accepting the unplanned pregnancy. The second is facing the decision of whether to abort, parent, or choose adoption. The third stage is getting used to the idea of adoption, if that is the choice, and facing your own stereotypes of what adoption means to you.

You and the birthmother may disagree about what the outcome of the pregnancy should be. This is one of those situations when meeting with a neutral party, such as a therapist, clergy, or family friend would be very helpful. In addition, it may be necessary to consult an adoption attorney or talk to a counselor at the adoption agency so they can inform you of your rights.

If you want to parent or participate fully in an adoption, you may need to take certain steps to ensure your rights. Some states require you to register with a "putative father registry." In addition, many states require you to financially and emotionally support the expectant mother and take a definitive step to claim the child, such as filing a claim with the courts shortly after birth. Other states will recognize your rights as a father if your name is on the birth certificate. It is important that you understand what you need to do to protect your rights.

Deciding on Adoption

Some birthfathers may initially disagree with the expectant mother's desire to proceed with an adoption plan. This resistance can be for a number of reasons. Friends and family may strongly influence them about what is "the right thing to do." Some men hope that a child might solidify or heal a shaky relationship. Other men believe that parenting their child is the consequence that they must live with for their part in the "mistake."

In addition to these objections, there are situations when birthfathers resist the adoption solely because the birthmother or adoption professionals exclude and disrespect them. When birthfathers threaten to disrupt or fight the adoption plan, the expectant mother, adoption professionals and prospective adoptive parents often perceive them as hostile and may not take the time to listen to their concerns.

The most difficult part about whether or not to consent to the adoption is that many times the situation requires the birthfather to make a quick decision. Once the shock of an unplanned pregnancy fades, it makes sense to focus your attention on whether you can be supportive of the expectant mother's decision.

You owe it to yourself and your child to explore your thoughts, feelings and life circumstances with someone who will not try to unduly influence you. An adoption attorney can answer your legal concerns. An adoption agency or counselor can help you explore the pros and cons of an adoption plan.

If you are in a relationship with the expectant mother, and even if you are not, let her know that you need some time to sort out your thoughts about the situation. Hopefully, it will soon become clear whether or not you are able to support an adoption plan and to what extent you want to be involved during the pregnancy and afterwards. After you have made your decision, consult with your attorney and/or adoption counselor about your next step.

If the Birthfather Would Rather Remain Anonymous

Some birthfathers will support the birthmother's decision to place their child for adoption by signing paperwork terminating their parental rights but will prefer no involvement in the adoption process. Others will avoid being identified at all and will refuse to sign the paperwork to terminate their rights. This will require the attorney or the adoptive family to go to court, after the birth of the baby, to have the birthfather's parental rights terminated.

A strong argument for the birthfather being active in the termination of his parental rights is because of the potential future impact on the child. When the child grows up and learns about his or her adoption, it can be reassuring to know that the birthfather participated voluntarily. If his or her adoptive parents have no history of the birthfather because he denied paternity or disappeared, the child might personalize the situation and feel bad. On the other hand, if the birthfather signs the papers and fills out the health history forms, the child will have proof that the birthfather cared enough to provide this important personal information.

How Involved can a Birthfather Become in the Adoption?

After you and the expectant mother agree to make an adoption plan, your level of involvement is for you to discuss with the expectant mother, prospective adoptive family, and your attorney or adoption professional. Some birthfathers work together with the expectant mothers all along the way. They help the expectant mother to pick the prospective adoptive family, attend meetings and get-togethers, go to doctor appointments and attend the hospital tour. They are usually present at the baby's birth and discuss ongoing contact with the prospective adoptive family.

Other birthfathers have much less involvement. They agree to sign the birthfather consent papers and provide medical information for the prospective adoptive family, but do not get actively involved in the adoption plans. Sometimes this is because the expectant mother does not want the birthfather to be involved; an adoption counselor can help you navigate this difficult situation so that you can participate fully in the adoption. The counselor can even facilitate a separate match meeting with the adoptive family and create an open adoption agreement that is separate from the expectant mother's agreement.

Even if you are involved in the pregnancy, the reality of the baby may take a while to sink in. Because you are one step removed from the baby, it may be difficult to imagine or prepare for what it will feel like when he or she actually arrives.

Some birthfathers begin to have intense feelings right away. Guilt, remorse, sadness, loss, and disappointment may begin during the pregnancy. Men sometimes feel they are "shirking their responsibilities" by not choosing to parent the baby. They fear the child will grow up resenting the decision and feeling angry at the birthfather for not trying harder to make it work. But, many birthfathers are finding that the open adoption is an alternative that allows them to provide crucial support to their birth child while allowing an adoption to move forward.

Open Adoption

Many birthfathers decide to fully participate in the adoption process through an open adoption. Usually birthfathers make this decision because they believe it is in the best interest of their birth child. This position is supported by research showing that children and adoptive families welcome birthfather participation in an open adoption.

Some birthfathers feel that they cannot be part of the adoption if they are no longer in a relationship with the birthmother, but this need not be the case. Sometimes birthparents who are no longer together can make an adoption plan together and even do joint visits with the adoptive family. More frequently in this situation, the birthfather and birthmother will have separate open adoption agreements with the adoptive family. These agreements are legally enforceable in twenty-three states for birthmothers and birthfathers, and most adoptive families will welcome a birthfather even if he is no longer in a relationship with the birthmother.

Children are eager to know their birthfathers and will want information about their birth families as well. Hearing their adoption story from a birthparent assures them that you made the adoption plan out of love. You can be honest about why you made this choice without fear that they will be angry or resent your decision. Perhaps the most important role you can play in their lives is to be a constant and reliable presence in their lives. Children need their birthfathers as much as they need their birthmothers so that they have all of the information about their birth families and can feel whole and complete.

"My father left my mother and me when I was only two. He just left one day, never looking back, never contacting us again. It has been so painful not knowing. Was it something about me? Whenever I think about my own son, Evan, I wonder, 'How can I do the same thing? How can I leave Evan like that?" But with the open adoption, I am not abandoning him. He knows who I am, and we have regular visits, and he gets to grow up in a family that can provide for him.

Jeremy, 19-year-old birthfather

Open adoption helps your birth child understand why you placed him for adoption and avoids feelings of abandonment as he or she grows up. You will have an opportunity to explain your dilemma to your birth child directly and let him or her know that you placed him or her for adoption because of circumstances in your life at the time, not because you did not love him or her. In addition, if the prospective adoptive family is able to meet you and get to know you, they will be in a much better position to represent you well to your birth child over the years and answer the child's questions honestly and lovingly.

Thinking over what is best for you, your child, and the expectant mother is not selfish. Some cultures, communities, and religions equate having children with being successful or powerful.

You may experience a lot of peer or family pressure to "face your responsibilities" or "keep the blood in the family." Just remember that the decision to parent has to fit *you* one hundred percent, not the people pressuring you to parent or not to parent. The adoption choice is definitely not the easy way out of an unplanned pregnancy, and it is not avoiding responsibility. In some ways, going through the adoption process is the most difficult option of all.

The Birth of the Baby

We have seen birthfathers become surprisingly emotional at the hospital when their child was born. As we mentioned before, you have been somewhat removed from the emotional rollercoaster of the anticipated adoption. You may have been feeling strong and solid during the pregnancy, but do not be surprised if you feel very out of control emotionally once the baby is born. Anticipate an onslaught of feelings and thoughts that have not previously surfaced.

Be sure that you and the birthmother have close, supportive people to talk with during this most difficult time. As a birthfather, you are an essential part of your child's adoption. You can be a very important support person for the birthmother. You can be reassuring and provide very critical information for the adoptive family. Finally, hearing of your involvement during this important time will communicate to your birth child that he or she was loved and valued from the beginning.

CHAPTER 11: THE OTHER IMPORTANT FAMILY MEMBERS

"My family didn't want me to place my baby for adoption at first. They thought I'd regret it."

Nora, 22-year-old birthmother

"They were very supportive of my decision throughout my pregnancy."

Mackenzie, 33-year-old birthmother

"I never told anyone in my family about the pregnancy or the adoption. They wouldn't understand. They would find a way to criticize me about the whole thing."

Grace, 18-year-old birthmother

Placing a child for adoption affects other members of the extended birth family in various ways and to varying degrees. Over the years, we have counseled many birth grandparents or other members of the extended birth family whose children, brothers, sisters, nieces, or nephews placed a baby for adoption. If you are the family member of a birthparent, you will experience many feelings about the adoption. You may want to talk to a counselor to help process your feelings.

Birth Grandparents (Parents of the Birthparents)

In most states, expectant mothers over the age of twelve do not need parental consent to place their baby for adoption. For parents whose child is pregnant and considering an adoption, your involvement will depend on the relationship you have with your child. Your role in the adoption plan may be distant and unclear. As much as you may want to have input, what your child needs most during this time is your unconditional support.

The losses for birth grandparents are many and complex. You may feel sadness at losing a grandchild, though many adoptive parents welcome birth grandparents for their child. You might also feel helpless because the choices your child faces are so profound. You may feel particularly angry and out of control. You may also feel proud of your child's ability to make a mature and thoughtful decision, whatever that decision is.

Sometimes a child will not tell her parents about the pregnancy or adoption plan. There are many reasons for this, including:

- Fear. She may not know how you will react and she expects a lot of anger.
- Shame. If your family does not talk about sexuality or birth control, your child may be ashamed to admit she is pregnant.
- Trauma. The pregnancy may be the result of incest or rape.
- Ignorance. Some birthparents do not realize they are pregnant until late in their pregnancy.
- Independence. Your child may want to do this on her own and worry that if she confides in you, you may try to sway her decision.

"Neither my parents nor my family knew I was pregnant. They found out the day she was born. They were in shock."

Isabella, 15-year-old birthmother

Tips for Birth Grandparents

If you discover your child is pregnant, there are some things you can do to make this incredibly difficult time a little bit easier for her and protect the quality of your relationship with her:

- First -- listen.
- Explore all of the options with your child. Offer to help find a qualified counselor.
- Communicate your point of view and support your child in hers.
- Give input when asked.
- Let your child make her own decisions about the pregnancy and delivery.
- Do not interfere with your child's relationship with the prospective adoptive family.
- Do not bad-mouth the birthfather.
- See a counselor if you need help coping with your child's decision.
- Try to find a "support" birth grandparent, someone who has been through this already. The adoption professional involved may have resources for you.
- Be kind to yourself. This is hard for you, too.

"My family was very supportive, and I could always talk to them about anything."

Leah, 16-year-old birthmother

"My family was torn between believing that I would actually do it and disbelief that I could be so 'cold.'"

Vicki, 25-year-old birthmother

Understanding and believing in adoption is a process. It takes a little getting used to and some education. If your child is contemplating participating in an open adoption, it will help you to become familiar with some of the current ideas about adoption.

There is a resource guide at the end of this book. In addition, many adoption agencies provide counseling and support services for birth grandparents.

One of the most difficult crisis periods in your child's life will be facing an unplanned pregnancy and deciding to place the baby for adoption. It is a time when she really needs your unconditional support. If you disagree with your child's plan and you cannot see yourself supporting her, you might miss out on an important opportunity to connect with her on a deep and profound level.

Brothers, Sisters and Other Relatives

"What is my relationship to this child?"

Donald, 26-year-old birth uncle

We have heard this and other questions from the extended family members of the birthparents. We have always believed that an emotional relationship exists among biological relatives, even though a legal relationship does not. However, it is very important to be sensitive to the expectant mother and prospective adoptive family and respect the relationship they have developed.

Some birthparents we have counseled chose not to have much contact with their birth child, but they have encouraged their extended family's involvement. Many adoptive families are very comfortable with these relationships, while a few are not and prefer all contact to go directly through the birthmother. If, as an extended family member, you desire some contact, speak to the birthparents about this and try to understand and respect their decisions.

"Everyone was very supportive . . . I don't know that I ever gave anyone the space to question my decision. I was so comfortable with it myself that I don't think they had any other choice. What I didn't find out until after I had signed the adoption

papers was that my family was ready to set up a nursery and help me raise my baby if I changed my mind. That they never let on really impressed me. Never once did anyone ever try to change or question my decision."

Samantha, 20-year-old birthmother

CHAPTER 12: CIRCUMSTANCES THAT REQUIRE ADDITIONAL THOUGHT, PLANNING AND COUNSELING

This chapter will briefly address adoption situations that merit special consideration and further exploration. Placing a child you have been parenting, making an adoption plan while incarcerated or considering surrogacy after adoption are special situations. In these cases, we strongly urge you to seek professionals who have a particular expertise in the area. There are, for example, adoption agencies that specialize in placements of older children.

Placing a Child You Have Been Parenting

Sometimes women parenting babies or young children call adoption agencies or attorneys asking about adoption. Most of these calls do not actually result in an adoptive placement, but are the desperate inquiries of women who feel at the end of their rope.

There are programs available for stressed-out parents, especially in urban areas, which offer respite care. Respite care is temporary care for those children whose parents feel overwhelmed with parenting and desperately need a break. Sometimes just a few hours a day away from your child will give you the down time you need to handle the stress. Your county Department of Social Services may be able to help you find respite care.

If, however, your parenting experience is getting harder and harder and you cannot cope or care for your child adequately, you might consider adoption. Counseling is essential if you are considering adoption for a child you have been parenting. If you call an adoption practitioner, an agency, or an attorney, ask them if you will receive as much counseling as you need. One session is not enough, and most reputable organizations will suggest several sessions before you even begin working on an adoption plan.

While making the decision, take some time to consider the vast implications a placement decision would have on you and your child. You can call the social services department in your community to see if you have the option of temporarily placing your child in a foster home to allow some respite while you are considering your options. If you are considering foster care, make sure you know what paperwork you will be required to sign and what legal issues are involved. If you have any concerns, ask an attorney to review the arrangement with you.

If you determine that an adoptive placement is in your child's best interest, finding an adoption provider and a prospective adoptive family is the next step. You should have a list of questions ready when you call an adoption agency or attorney.

Sample Questions for Older Child Placements

- Do you do placements of older children?
- How much counseling can I receive before and after the placement?
- Do you have foster care?
- How long after the placement will I have before I must sign the papers to terminate my parental rights?
- Will I be able to have ongoing visits with my baby or child after I place him or her with the adoptive family?
- How will you handle the transition of my child to the adoptive family?
- Will my child go immediately from my home to the adoptive family's home?
- What can I do to prepare my child for the transition?
- How can I prepare my other children?

Most adoption professionals agree that the transfer of a child from one family to another should happen slowly. Perhaps you and your child can spend time with the prospective adoptive family in your home, and on other types of outings. Then perhaps a series of sleepovers that slowly lengthen the time the child spends with the prospective adoptive family.

Although a slow transition may feel tremendously painful for you once you have made up your mind to place, children fare better when you ease them into a change of this magnitude. Your adoption professional can work with you and the prospective adoptive family to help your child through this process and guide you through this difficult and period.

Making an Adoption Plan While Incarcerated

Women incarcerated in prison or jail can make an adoption plan, even an open adoption plan, but it does take planning and perseverance. If you are incarcerated and want to explore adoption, you should talk to the jail or prison social worker and ask him or her for assistance in locating an adoption agency or attorney. If this is not possible or he or she cannot help you, you can call an adoption agency or attorney (most will accept collect calls from a jail or prison) and ask if they will send a social worker to come talk to you. You will probably need to put the name of the social worker on your visitor's list. The social worker will be discreet about the nature of the visit.

Once you make a final decision that you want to proceed with an adoption plan, the social worker will need to coordinate with the authorities at the jail or prison to ensure that the adoption proceeds as planned. She may be able to arrange for you to meet with the adoptive family before you give birth so you can have a match meeting, but this is not always possible.

In any case, she will talk to you and the prospective adoptive family about the hospital plan and contact after placement, but all of these arrangements will be contingent on what the jail or prison authorities will allow. Usually the authorities are cooperative, but sometimes they have their own biases for and against adoption, so you must prepare yourself for both supportive and critical reactions.

Most adoption agencies can provide counseling while you are in jail or prison. Usually these sessions are conducted as part of a regular visit, as most jails or prisons will not provide a private room for adoption counseling. Although this is not ideal, most incarcerated expectant women feel that counseling is important for them in deciding if adoption is the right plan and in helping them to deal with the grief after placement.

If you give birth while incarcerated, the jail or prison will take you to a local hospital for the birth. Sometimes they will allow the adoptive parents to be in the room if you wish, but often they will not allow anyone except for the health professionals in the room. Nevertheless, the adoptive family you choose can come to the hospital and be available to take the baby home, or care for him or her in the hospital, if needed.

The adoption professional will send the hospital plan to the hospital if possible, but it is important to memorize the phone numbers of the prospective adoptive parents and the adoption agency. That way you can give this information to the nurses and doctors attending to you, if necessary. Sometimes the jail or prison will not cooperate because they feel that they might be coercing you into a decision, and they want to be clear that they are neutral on the subject of adoption. Hospital personnel will usually contact either the adoptive family or the adoption agency if you tell them you have made an adoption plan.

If you are likely to be in jail or prison when you give birth, tell your adoption professional. She will understand and try to complete the required arrangements before your incarceration so you have less to worry about while you serve your time and wait for the birth.

"The guards would not let the adoptive parents into my room during or after the birth, but the doctor told me they were right next door and sent their love. I cuddled my baby for thirty

minutes, and then they took her to the adoptive parents. It was a relief to know she would be safe and that I knew exactly who she was with. They even visited with the baby several times during my jail time, and now that I am free we are in regular contact."

Camilla, 22-year-old birthmother

"I was embarrassed to meet the adoptive parents while I was in prison, but they were so nice, I quickly forgot the circumstances. We talked until the last minute of the visiting time. The adoptive father was a sheriff's deputy, so he really understood how things worked inside, which made me comfortable because I didn't have to explain everything to them. The guards even let them in the room when I gave birth. Now that I am out, they are still so supportive."

Lillianna, 25-year-old birthmother

Becoming a Surrogate after Placing for Adoption

Sometimes a birthmother will subsequently agree to serve as a surrogate for the adoptive family who is parenting her birth child. As a surrogate, you would carry and give birth to a baby that may, or may not, be genetically related to you. Some surrogates use their own eggs, which doctors fertilize with sperm from the adoptive father or a donor. Other surrogates carry babies conceived with eggs and sperm from the adoptive family or egg and/or sperm from donors. If you use your own eggs, you would be the biological mother of the child.

Surrogacy is not adoption, and there is a completely different set of rules regulating it. These are outside our area of expertise, but we would like you to take a few minutes to think about all of the possible reasons you might be considering surrogacy.

In most cases, a birthmother will make the suggestion to the adoptive parents when she sees they are struggling to build their family. Birthmothers usually make this offer because they want to help the adoptive family, but there are often unconscious motivations as well. For example, do you feel indebted to the family for parenting your birth child or do you want the adoptive family to feel indebted to you for providing them with all of their children? Are you worried that if the family adopts a second time that you will have to share their attention with another birthmother? Do you miss how much attention you got from the adoptive family during the adoption process and hope that the surrogacy process will replicate that experience? Do you feel like a planned pregnancy would offset or redeem you because of your previously unplanned pregnancy? There may also be financial motivations as families usually pay surrogates for their services.

Although most birthmothers are primarily motivated by their desire to help the adoptive family, they usually have a combination of motivations. There is nothing wrong with having other reasons for wanting to be a surrogate, but it is wise to examine all of your motivations before moving forward, just to be sure that you are comfortable with making this decision. You may want to talk to a counselor before making a final commitment.

It is never appropriate for the adoptive family to ask you to be a surrogate. This puts everyone in an awkward position. If this happens to you, please consult your adoption provider to see if they can help you discuss this with the adoptive family.

CHAPTER 13: ADOPTION PLANNING IF YOU ARE LESBIAN OR TRANSGENDER

Lesbians have unplanned pregnancies, as do transgender men. Lesbian women and transgender men also place children for adoption. Sometimes lesbians and transgender men feel that they will be ridiculed or misunderstood if they want to make an adoption plan, but in our experience there are adoption providers and adoptive families who are sensitive to and supportive of lesbian and transgender birthparents.

It is important that you find an adoption provider that understands the unique issues you face as a lesbian or transgender man making an adoption plan. Adoption attorneys, agencies or facilitators who regularly work with LGBT adoptive families are probably the best adoption providers for lesbians and transgender men who are considering adoption. It is easy to make this assessment by visiting the website of the provider and noting if they are welcoming to LGBT adoptive families.

Transgender Men

Transgender men[4] with unplanned pregnancies can find the experience of pregnancy and adoption planning alienating because our culture defines the pregnancy and adoption experience as a female one. Everything is set up with the assumption that the

---

[4] Transgender man: people who were assigned female at birth but identify and live as men may use this term to describe themselves. They may shorten it to trans man. (Note: trans man, not "transman.") Some may also use FTM, an abbreviation for female-to-male. www.glaad.org/reference/transgender

person giving birth is female, even though the person may not have a female gender identity.

As stated earlier, it is important to work with an adoption attorney, agency or facilitator who understands the issues a transgender man will face in adoption. You should be able to find one by looking at the websites of providers and noting which ones are LGBT-friendly. The next step is to find an adoptive family who will be a good parent or parents for your child. Clearly, your definition of "good parent or parents" will include a family that respects and is comfortable with your gender identity and expression.

Many of the transgender men we work with choose other members of the LGBT community to parent their children. Lesbian, gay male or transgender adoptive parents are often a good choice when they are aware of and supportive of the issues facing transgender people. However this is not always the case.

Many heterosexual people are also educated about and supportive of transgender people, so you may want to consider heterosexual adoptive families, as well. If you are unsure if a family is open to working with you due to your gender identity, ask your adoption counselor to screen families for you.

One of the first issues you will want to address is the language used to describe your role. Do you want the adoption professionals, prospective adoptive parents and ultimately your birth child to call you "birthmother," "birthfather," "birthparent" or something else entirely?

Pronouns are another challenge. Some transgender men prefer "he/him" while others favor a gender-neutral pronoun like "ze/zir." Other times transgender men have shared that they do not care about language as long as people are respectful of their gender identity. We understand this feeling, since parsing language can feel like an indulgence when there is hatred and discrimination against transgender people.

An adoption plan, however, can be an opportunity to think about and say what your preferences are and to have other people affirm and respect your choices about your gender identity. Ultimately it is your choice about which words you want the adoption professionals and adoptive family to use to describe you. Your adoption counselor will raise this issue for discussion during the match meeting (see Chapter 3).

It will be especially important for your adoption counselor to ensure that the hospital is respectful of your gender identity during the birth and that the counselor and the prospective adoptive family are ready and able to advocate for your needs, if any issue should arise during the hospital stay.

"I was really worried that everyone would judge me because I was male, but the adoptive parents were wonderful, and my adoption counselor made sure the hospital staff treated me well. My birth daughter calls me by my first name, Jon, and her parents call me her birthparent. I thought my gender identity would be a big problem in an adoption, but this has not been the case."

Jon, 19-year-old birthparent

Lesbians

Lesbian women with unplanned pregnancies often feel alienated from their community. Many people view this situation as an aberration, and lesbian women dealing with an unplanned pregnancy can face an unusual level of isolation. Some, perhaps all, of their friends may not understand how this could have happened and may even question if they are really a lesbian. Although unplanned pregnancies are less common for lesbian than for heterosexual women, they do happen more frequently than most people think.

The first step is to ensure that you work with an adoption professional that understands your situation, and has experience working with lesbians considering adoption. The best advice is to work with an agency, attorney or facilitator that regularly works with LGBT adoptive families.

Sometimes lesbian women want to place with an LGBT adoptive family so that their child will grow up in a home that is LGBT-friendly. Other times lesbians feel so alienated from the LGBT community that they will only consider placing with a heterosexual family. Fortunately, there are LGBT and heterosexual families that will be understanding and supportive of your situation and provide a LGBT-friendly environment for your birth child.

You can ask your adoption counselor to screen families for you if you are concerned that families might be judgmental about your sexual orientation. Your adoption counselor and the adoptive family can also advocate for your needs at the hospital, as most hospitals assume women giving birth are heterosexual, even though this is outdated thinking.

"I really put myself through the wringer once I found out I was pregnant, but I knew I wanted to make an adoption plan with a family who would be accepting of me as a lesbian. As it turned out, I met both LGBT and heterosexual adoptive families who did accept me. I chose a gay male couple to parent my son, but I think some of the heterosexual families would have provided LGBT-friendly homes as well."

Maddie, 27-year-old birthmother

If you are married to a female partner or you are in committed partnership that you view as a marriage, your wife or partner may have equal rights to the child. A spouse is the legal parent of any child born to either partner during the marriage even if they are not the biological parent. In some states, an unmarried partner who provides financial and emotional support to the biological mother is also considered a legal parent. This is especially true if you list them as a parent on the birth certificate. Many states allow birth certificates to list two parents of the same sex.

A legal parent must agree to the adoption. You cannot proceed with an adoption without the consent of all the legal parents of the child. If your wife or partner wants the adoption to proceed she will need to agree to have her parental rights terminated. As of the printing of this book, most states have not yet developed the standard paperwork required to terminate the rights of two parents of the same sex, but agencies and attorneys can get an order from the court to do so. It is important to work with an agency or attorney who understands this process, and the rights of same-sex legal parents so this process is completed correctly.

Gender Identity and Sexual Orientation in Adoption

Sexual orientation and gender identity should not be barriers for men and women considering adoption. Unfortunately, this is not always the case because of outdated assumptions and stereotypes. However, if you work with supportive adoption professionals and prospective adoptive parents, the adoption process should be affirmative of your gender identity and sexual orientation.

Finally, it is important to remember that your experience is not unusual or shameful. You have a right to make an adoption plan and to feel that the professionals and adoptive families are supportive and respectful.

CHAPTER 14: CLOSING THOUGHTS

The journey from discovering you are pregnant to placing your child for adoption can be long and arduous but also filled with hope and joy. Although some expectant mothers ultimately decide this is not the right path for them, most birthmothers who place their babies with an adoptive family find a sense of pride and accomplishment in their decision.

Adoption is not an easy choice. It requires a mixture of determination, patience, willingness to take risks, and vulnerability to emotions. We sincerely hope we have been able to provide you with understanding, knowledge, and most importantly, practical tools that you can use along your journey.

We hope you will find peace with your decision.

CHAPTER 15: RESEARCH ON OPEN ADOPTION

There has been significant research done on open adoption over the last twenty years. It includes three long-term studies on the outcomes for children, birthparents and adoptive parents in open adoptions. One is a small, qualitative study and the other two are large-sample research projects. All three studies started data collection in the late 1980s and early 1990s. The findings of all three studies are strikingly similar.

The largest and most important study is the Minnesota/Texas Adoption Research Project (MTARP). The principal investigators are Dr. Harold Grotevant and Dr. Ruth McCoy. Their research finds that open adoption is in the best interest of the adoptee, birthparents and adoptive parents. This confirms a hypothesis advocated since 1976 by open adoption pioneers such as Kathleen Silber, IAC's associate executive director.

As we discussed in the introduction, before the 1980s adoption professionals promoted closed adoption because they believed that open adoption would be confusing to the child, delay healing for the birthparents, and inhibit full parenting by the adoptive parents. Dr. Grotevant and Dr. McCoy's research convincingly dispels all of these myths. Adoptees are not confused by open adoption. Any dissatisfaction they felt was because they wanted more contact with their birth families, not less.

According to Dr. Grotevant, "Frequency of contact can vary from initial contacts made only around the time of the adoptive placement to frequent, ongoing contact. Frequency typically ebbs and flows over time as circumstances change, and contacts can include the adopted child with any combination of adoptive and birth family members. Our key finding about adopted children is that their *perception* of the contact, especially their satisfaction with it, is more important than how often they have contact or what type of contact they have. In general, children who had contact were more satisfied with arrangements than those who did not. When family members were dissatisfied with their contact, it was almost always because they wanted more (rather than less) contact but were unable to bring it about. It was this satisfaction, rather than the actual level of contact, that predicted better adjustment among adopted adolescents and young adults."

The research also shows birthparents in open adoptions are most satisfied with their adoptions and have less unresolved grief later in life. Dr. Grotevant states, "Birth mothers in open adoptions who were more satisfied with their contact arrangements had less unresolved grief 12-20 years after the placements than those involved in closed adoptions. Birth mothers typically don't want to take on a parenting role. In fact, it's clear that the adoptive parents are the full parents of the child, but birthmothers are often comforted by having information about and some contact with their children, knowing that they are safe and doing well, and having the reassurance that their decision to place the child for adoption was a good one."

Finally, the research confirmed that adoptive parents in open adoptions had the least fear about parenting or birthparents wanting to reclaim their child. According to Dr. Grotevant, "Adoptive parents were least afraid in open adoptions, often because the birth and adoptive parents had had a conversation about this issue and the birth mothers would often say, 'Why would I take my child back? I placed my child with you. I just want to make sure that my child is OK.' In closed adoptions, where adoptive mothers knew little about a child's birth mother, fears tended to grow out of negative stereotypes about birth parents that were not informed by reality."

Although the conclusions noted above from Dr. Grotevant and Dr. McCoy's research are based on voluntary infant adoption in the United States, Dr. Grotevant also noted, "In the United Kingdom, most adoptions take place through the public care system, after children have been removed from their birth parents because of neglect, abuse, or parental incapacity. The UK research suggests that open adoption can work well even where children have been taken away from birth parents, although sometimes contact may be with birth grandparents or birth siblings rather than with the birth parents." This indicates that open adoption may also be a good option for adoptions facilitated through the foster care system in the United States.

In any case, the research is convincing that open adoption is the best option for the vast majority of adoptees, birthparents and adoptive parents. However, according to Dr. Grotevant, "Managing contact over time requires participants' flexibility, communication skills, ability to maintain boundaries, and commitment to the relationships. These skills can be learned, and they can be supported by others, through informal, psycho-educational, and therapeutic means." This means that it is important to work with adoption professionals who can help with the process.

The quotes above from Dr. Grotevant were taken from his blog about his and Dr. McCoy's open adoption research. To find out more about Dr. Grotevant and Dr. McCoy's research on open adoption please read their blog at http://childandfamilyblog.com/open-adoption-2/.

CHAPTER 16: RESOURCE GUIDE

SUPPORT GROUPS

National:
Birthmom Buds: www.birthmombuds.com
Birthmom Buds provides mentors, friendship and support to women considering adoption. They host retreats and other supportive events for birthmothers and women considering adoption.

California:
On Your Feet Foundation—California: www.onyourfeetca.org
On Your Feet Foundation in California provides mentors, counselors, academic scholarships and retreats for birthmothers in California.

Illinois and Indiana:
On Your Feet Foundation—Illinois and Indiana: www.oyff.org
On Your Feet Foundation in Illinois and Indiana provides case management, coaching, monetary grants, retreats and community for birthparents.

BOOKS

(Available from Amazon.com and other suppliers)

Open Adoption:
"Because I Loved You: A Birthmother's View of Open Adoption"
Patricia Dischler weaves her own story of how she placed her son in a closed adoption and how opening the adoption allowed her to heal herself from the legal and emotional aspects of placing a child.

"Making Room in Our Hearts: Keeping Family Ties Through Open Adoption" {XE: "Making Room in Our Hearts"} *by Micky Duxbury*
This book is a great discussion of openness in adoption. It is extremely well written with open adoption stories used to illustrate the author's points.

"True Stories of Open Adoption (Volume I)"
In an effort to educate the general population and prospective birth and adoptive parents, the Independent Adoption Center has compiled true stories of open adoption from past clients and staff members who agreed to share in their own words how their families came to be. These stories will touch the reader while showing the depth of these distinctive relationships.

For Children:
"Sam's Sister"
This is a picture book for young children about a birth parent who places a baby for adoption while continuing to parent another young child.

ABOUT THE AUTHORS

Jennifer Bliss, Psy.D., L.C.S.W., L.P.C.C.

Jennifer Bliss is the national associate counseling director and Los Angeles branch director of the Independent Adoption Center. She is in charge of training open adoption counselors, the social workers who provide services to birthparents and adoptive parents as they navigate the open adoption process.

Dr. Bliss previously worked with a California county child protective services unit and has spent the last decade working for the Independent Adoption Center. She has a Bachelor of Arts from the University of Southern California, a Master of Social Work from the University of California at Los Angeles, and a Doctor of Psychology in clinical psychology from Ryokan College.

Ann Wrixon, M.S.W., M.B.A.

Ann Wrixon is the executive director of the Independent Adoption Center. She succeeded IAC founder Dr. Bruce Rappaport when he retired in August 2006. During her tenure, the IAC has more than doubled the number of families for whom it provides services.

Ms. Wrixon has spent her career managing non-profit organizations dedicated to improving education and child welfare.

She has published widely on those subjects, as well as on many adoption-related topics, including open adoption, LGBT adoption and interstate adoption. Ms. Wrixon has a Bachelor of Arts from Rutgers University, a Master of Business Administration from San Francisco State University, and a Master of Social Work from California State University East Bay.

ABOUT THE INDEPENDENT ADOPTION CENTER

Founded in 1982, the mission of the Independent Adoption Center (IAC) is to provide open adoption placement and counseling to birth and adoptive families to ensure that every child grows up feeling loved and supported.

IAC fulfills its mission by providing the following services:

- IAC informs, supports, and guides birth and adoptive parents through the process of creating healthy new families through open adoption.
- IAC's professional staff provides support and counseling for birthparents, works closely with adoptive parents throughout the adoption process, and provides ongoing post-placement support and consultation for birthparents and adoptive families.
- IAC focuses on transforming lives through open adoption by serving the best interests of birthparents, children, and adoptive families.
- IAC is one of the few adoption agencies in the country that has never had any exclusionary policies for adoptive parents, including age, sexual orientation, gender identity or expression, marital status, religion, ethnic background, color, or race.

The IAC is a licensed adoption agency in California, Connecticut, Florida, Georgia, Indiana, North Carolina, New York, and Texas. You can find more information about IAC at www.iheartadoption.org or www.adoptionhelp.org or by calling 1-800-877-6736.

Made in the USA
San Bernardino, CA
03 September 2016